THE
TURNAROUND

By Darrin Donnelly

THINK LIKE A WARRIOR
The Five Inner Beliefs That Make You Unstoppable

OLD SCHOOL GRIT
Times May Change, But the Rules for Success Never Do

RELENTLESS OPTIMISM
How a Commitment to Positive Thinking Changes Everything

LIFE TO THE FULLEST
A Story About Finding Your Purpose and Following Your Heart

VICTORY FAVORS THE FEARLESS
How to Defeat the 7 Fears That Hold You Back

THE TURNAROUND
How to Build Life-Changing Confidence

THE
TURNAROUND

HOW TO BUILD
LIFE-CHANGING CONFIDENCE

Darrin Donnelly

Sports for the Soul

Stories of Faith, Family, Courage, and Character.

This book is part of the *Sports for the Soul* series. For updates on this book, future books, and a free newsletter that delivers advice and inspiration from top coaches, athletes, and sports psychologists, join us at: **SportsForTheSoul.com**.

The *Sports for the Soul* newsletter will help you:
- Find your calling and follow your passion
- Harness the power of positive thinking
- Build your self-confidence
- Attack every day with joy and enthusiasm
- Develop mental toughness
- Increase your energy and stay motivated
- Explore the spiritual side of success
- Be a positive leader for your family and your team
- Become the best version of yourself
- And much more…

Join us at: **SportsForTheSoul.com**.

To Laura, Patrick, Katie, and Tommy;

who are everything to me.

Introduction

"People with confident, optimistic outlooks tend to succeed. People who are pessimistic, who lack confidence, tend to fail."

– Dr. Bob Rotella, World-Renowned Sports Psychologist

Confidence is essential to success, happiness, and peace of mind. If we don't believe we can accomplish something, we won't. If we don't feel good about ourselves, we won't be happy. If we don't believe in ourselves, we'll never be at peace with who we are and what we're capable of.

Yet, sometimes it seems like right when we most need a boost of self-confidence, it is nowhere to be found.

We've all been there. Those times when it feels like life is working against us. When we have a losing season, we face a financial or health crisis, we lose a job, or we just seem to be encountering one big problem after another.

It's during those tough times when we often lose our self-confidence, which only makes matters worse. We start doubting ourselves, questioning whether we will get back on our feet, wondering how we will ever turn things around.

This book will show you how to build and maintain confidence no matter what is going on around you – in good times and in bad.

No matter how dire the situation, every turnaround starts with renewed self-confidence. It is the catalyst for getting back up, conquering your problems, and feeling good about yourself again.

A person will tend to perform up to (or down to) his or her self-image and the person with a confident, positive self-image will outperform the person with an insecure, negative self-image in pretty much every area of life. That is why confidence plays such a vital role in the type of life you live.

The most confident team usually ends up winning the game. The most confident salesperson usually leads his or her team in sales. The most confident leaders tend to lead the most successful organizations.

Confidence plays a crucial role in our personal lives as well. Self-confident people feel good about themselves. They have healthier relationships. They worry less. They enjoy life more.

But despite knowing how important confidence is, we also know how fickle it can be. Coaches will tell you that one of the questions they most often hear from athletes is, "How can I build more confidence?"

Self-doubt and insecurity hold so many of us back from

the success we desire.

Many people have surrendered to the false belief that confidence only comes *after* success — not realizing how important it is to build confidence *first* in order to succeed at a higher level. Others have come to believe they just aren't the "confident type" — as though confidence is something genetically given to only a select few in this world.

The fact is, confidence can and *must* be generated from within if you want to be successful.

Not only is a healthy level of self-confidence required for success, but it's also necessary for your well-being. Happiness and peace of mind will always be fleeting if you're wracked with self-doubt and insecurity.

Adding to the challenge of acquiring confidence is the fact that confidence can be a tricky thing to quantify. How much is enough? People sometimes worry about becoming *too* confident and therefore err on the side of timidity.

This book will teach you how to build a healthy level of confidence and eliminate the self-doubt that holds you back.

Like all books in the *Sports for the Soul* series, this is an inspirational fable. It's a story written from the perspective of a man looking back at the confidence-building lessons he learned as a college football player three decades ago — lessons that carried him to success and happiness well beyond the football field.

Once an insecure fourth-string quarterback on one of the worst college football teams in America, Danny O'Connor's life changes when a new coach named Bud Sullivan is hired and begins showing Danny and his teammates how to build the confidence they need to turn around their losing ways.

Over the course of three years, Bud lays the foundation for one of the greatest turnarounds in college football history and Danny learns invaluable lessons that will last him a lifetime.

As this story plays out, you will learn important truths about the role confidence plays in your life along with the practical, real-world methods used by some of the greatest coaches of all time for instantly generating self-confidence.

Confidence-building is an ongoing process and the techniques in this book—when used regularly—will generate the type of confidence that can turn around any situation and ignite winning streaks in every area of your life.

Darrin Donnelly
SportsForTheSoul.com

THE TURNAROUND

1

"The man who views the world at fifty the same as he did at twenty has wasted thirty years of his life."

– Muhammad Ali, 3-Time World Heavyweight Champion

Friday Afternoon, August 30, 2019

Thirty years.

Thirty years.

There's no way it has been that long.

I won't go so far as to use that tired cliché about it feeling "just like yesterday." The graying of my hair, the crow's feet around my eyes, the fact that I haven't run a forty-yard dash in, well, thirty years — it all reminds me I'm not in college anymore.

But I'm not an old man either.

Am I?

Ten years removed from the glory days of college feels about right. *Maybe* twenty. But not thirty. No way.

Yet, here I am, walking through the campus quad, just

like I did nearly every day three decades ago, only this time I'm not late for class or on my way to the football facility. I'm strolling along with Sherry, my wife of twenty-nine years.

The main reason for this trip is tomorrow's football game and the thirty-year reunion of the 1989 Arkansas A&M football team. I was the senior quarterback on that team and many of my old teammates are meeting for a tailgate party before the game. At halftime, we'll walk out onto the field and wave to the crowd. I'm looking forward to catching up with several of the guys I haven't seen in years.

The fall semester at Arkansas A&M University has already started and though it's getting late in the day on a Friday, it's still lively here at the center of campus. The busiest place is the Student Union, a building four times the size it was when I was a student here. We'll make our way over there shortly—there's an impressive campus bookstore inside packed with all the Bulldog apparel a visiting alumnus could ask for.

Sherry grabs my arm and pulls us off the sidewalk path when she notices a freed-up stone bench underneath a large shade tree.

"Let's take a seat," she says. "I want to enjoy the view for a minute."

I sit next to her and notice she is smiling big.

"Takes you back, doesn't it?" I say.

"It really does." She squeezes my hand. We both spent five years as students here. The memories come rushing back.

It's a typically hot and humid late-summer day in Joline, Arkansas, and it's nice to take a seat in the shade. A strong breeze blowing through the big green trees on campus cools the sweat on my forehead. From the bench, Sherry and I enjoy the campus scene.

Many students have gathered in groups, telling stories and laughing. Some have staked out an area of freshly-cut grass where they're lying down to read books or just enjoy the sunshine. A few couples walk tightly together, not necessarily hand-in-hand—maybe that's not a thing anymore?—but close enough to make it clear they're together. A handful of professor types engage in conversations with students or with each other—nothing too serious, lots of smiles and laughs; it's too early in the semester for stressed-out students or faculty squabbles.

Everyone looks happy. And excited. Even those students who are more purposefully hurrying along or typing away on their phones have smiles (or at least hints of a smile) on their faces.

First exams are still a couple weeks off and there's unbridled hope in the atmosphere—that feeling that a new year is upon us and anything is possible. It doesn't hurt that today is the Friday afternoon of Labor Day weekend—a three-day weekend that just happens to include the first football game of the season on Saturday.

The vibe is infectious and I can't help but grin as I inhale and take it all in.

College.

There's nothing like those days. They go by fast.

Too fast.

Arkansas A&M will host Vanderbilt tomorrow in the season-opener. The Bulldogs are expected to win, but you never know how those first games are going to go.

I think back to my days as a player here. That nervousness mixed with excitement and adrenaline in the days, hours, and moments before a game. I think of that old, dingy locker room—nothing like the plush new facilities players enjoy these days. I think of sitting on that wooden bench in our locker room, my foot tapping incessantly on the concrete floor as kickoff approached. I think of Bud Sullivan giving us one of his fired-up speeches before taking the field.

Bud Sullivan. The man is now a coaching legend, a member of the College Football Hall of Fame. He would coach Arkansas A&M for twenty-one seasons and win a National Championship along the way. But when he was first announced as our head coach, none of us had ever heard of him.

I was lucky to be a part of those first teams with Bud as the coach. What if he hadn't been hired here? My life would have turned out completely different.

Bud took over one of the worst college football programs in the country and taught us how to win. He taught us that winning begins within. He taught us that winners see themselves differently. He taught us that how you see yourself determines your level of success or failure in *every* area of life. He taught us how to believe in ourselves. He taught us the importance of self-confidence.

No matter how dire or difficult things have sometimes gotten in my life, I've always been able to rely on the lessons Bud taught us.

They have never let me down.

What I learned in the three years with Bud Sullivan as my coach (and the thirty years since) equipped me to chase my biggest dreams and live my life to the fullest. He taught me what it means to develop true confidence, not fake confidence. He showed me how confidence can instantly ignite a turnaround in any difficult situation. He trained me to see how my focus and expectations determine my experiences. He taught me that no matter how difficult a situation gets, there is *always* a way to turn things around if I truly believe in myself.

Thirty years of life experience after my time here have only reinforced the truth of the lessons he taught me and everyone else on our team.

I shake my head. Unreal to think three decades have passed since I went to school here. Thirty years ago this week, I was walking this very quad and just starting my final year at Arkansas A&M.

"I know this sounds crazy, but I don't feel like it's been *that* long since we were students here," Sherry says, echoing my exact thoughts. "Remember how excited we were about what the future might bring?"

I nod, remembering those feelings. Being on campus, the nostalgia is thick and I *feel* those feelings boiling up inside. The feeling that anything is possible and you've got your whole life in front of you.

I think back to my days here. The fun we had and the excitement I felt, the music of the '80s (hair bands, Springsteen, and a new thing called rap), the football of the '80s (the wishbone offense, giant shoulder pads, and the old Southwest Conference), laughing with guys who would become lifelong friends, walking in the quad with my future wife, bonding with my teammates as we battled through grueling two-a-day practices in the oppressive summer heat, and backyard parties running late into the night during the offseason—something that now sounds exhausting to me.

I chuckle to myself as the memories come flooding back.

But then I remember the dark times. The bad path I was headed down. The self-doubt, the cynicism, and the humiliation I felt.

A year-and-a-half into my college career, I wanted to quit and never come back to this place. I was actually *embarrassed* to be a college football player here. Pretty much everybody on the team was.

That's when Bud Sullivan showed up and the turnaround began. The turnaround for our team — one of the most impressive turnarounds in college football history — but also the turnaround in my life.

I would not be living the life I now love living if it had not been for Coach Bud Sullivan.

That, I am sure of.

2

"I think a coach has every right to be demanding – and should be demanding – but you've got no right to be demeaning to another person."

– R.C. Slocum, Hall of Fame College Football Coach

1986

Two months before I had ever heard of Bud Sullivan, I suffered through the most embarrassing afternoon of my life.

It was a dreary early-November Saturday back in 1986. I was in my second year at Arkansas A&M. This was long before I was known to sports fans across America as Dan O'Connor, host of *The Dan O'Connor Show* – a nationally-syndicated sports talk radio show. Back then, the few who knew me by name called me *Danny* O'Connor. To most, I was just a nameless scout-team quarterback who never saw the field.

At least, that's what I was before that dreadful Saturday

when I did finally enter a game.

I had redshirted during my first season (a technique used by college programs to save players a season of eligibility if they're not good enough to play during their first year with the program), which made me a "redshirt freshman" for the '86 season. I spent most the year as the scout-team quarterback (the guy who ran the opposing team's offense in practice), battling for the fourth-team spot on one of the worst college football teams in the country. Through a stroke of luck—very *bad* luck, as it would turn out—I was thrown in as the starting QB for our home game against Rice University on this particular Saturday.

Here's how it happened.

Earlier in the week, our first-team QB injured his shoulder in practice and the team doctor said he'd have to miss the Rice game. A week before that, our second-team QB quit the team. And a week before that, our third-team QB got kicked off the team. Heading into our eighth game of the season, I was promoted above Mike Pederson, the guy who had been fourth on the depth chart most of the season. He was a true freshman and our coach, Wade Wyatt, didn't want to burn his redshirt—especially when our 1-6 record up to that point had already guaranteed us another losing season near the bottom of the conference standings.

Our stadium was only about one-quarter full when Rice came to town. The Owls were 2-6 and both our teams were trying to stay out of last place in the old Southwest Conference (SWC).

This was supposed to be our best chance to pick up a conference win—something that hadn't happened in four years for Arkansas A&M. But thanks to my epically horrendous performance that afternoon, the only thing we would win was the race to see which one of our teams could reach seven losses first.

Just before I ran onto the field for my first collegiate start, Coach Wyatt grabbed me by the arm, gave me a fierce look, and said, "We're all counting on you. *Do not* screw this up."

I nodded and gulped simultaneously. I ran out to the huddle and called the first play. We broke the huddle and I walked to the line of scrimmage with shaky legs telling myself, *I'm not ready for this. I'm not ready for this. Don't screw up. Don't screw up.*

On the first snap of my first game as the starting quarterback, I fumbled the ball and Rice recovered on our seventeen-yard line. They scored a touchdown three plays later.

My second play of the game, I threw an interception that Rice returned for a touchdown.

A few plays later, I threw another interception.

In the second quarter, I fumbled the ball into our end zone and Rice recovered it for a touchdown.

In one half of play, I completed just one pass in nine

attempts (for a gain of three yards), fumbled the ball twice, and threw two interceptions as I led our team to a 28-0 halftime deficit.

Coach Wyatt, wearing his giant trademark cowboy hat and with his deep, slow, two-packs-a-day smokers' drawl, addressed the team at halftime by saying, "Needless to say, we'll be going with the other guy at quarterback in the second half."

The "other guy" was Pederson, the true freshman I was promoted in front of prior to the game. Apparently, burning his redshirt on a game we were destined to lose was worth it if it meant putting an end to my embarrassing performance.

Without me in there, the team played better, but I had dug us too deep of a hole. We lost, 38-14.

Standing on the sidelines during the second half of the game, I wanted to hide from the world. I couldn't wait for the game to end. Only one teammate dared to say a word to me. To the rest, it was like I was contagious and my teammates didn't want to be infected with whatever was making me play so horribly.

Brian Dawson, my roommate and our team's starting linebacker, was the only guy who talked to me. Midway through the fourth quarter, he slapped me on the back of my pads and said, "Look at it this way, Danny Boy, it can't get any worse."

With a stone face, I turned to Brian and saw his big grin

quickly fade away.

"Too early, I get it," he said as he put his helmet on and walked away.

After the game, Coach Wyatt gave what little self-esteem I had left one final knockout blow. He walked up to me, looked me in the eye, and said, loud enough for half the locker room to hear, "Well, congratulations, Danny. You took the one chance this team had at turning things around and blew it for us. But if you think you feel bad, think of how I feel. I'm the idiot who recruited you. You don't belong at this level, son, and you never did."

Talk about a punch to the gut.

Actually, a punch to the gut would've felt better and its lingering effects would not have lasted as long.

Wyatt walked away shaking his head and he never said another word to me.

Literally.

From that point on, he barely looked my direction at practice and I didn't see another down of playing time the rest of the season.

Not that I *wanted* to play another down. I spent the next few weeks of practice with my eyes low and my mouth shut, doing the bare minimum I could get away with as the scout-team quarterback. I didn't want to make any more mistakes that would lead to ridicule from Wyatt or my position coach.

The Saturday after Thanksgiving, we lost to Arkansas,

55-0. Wyatt was fired moments after the clock hit 0:00 in our final game of the season, a loss that gave us a record of 1-10 and another last-place finish in the SWC.

The 1986 season marked the eighth-straight year the Arkansas A&M Bulldogs finished either last or next to last in the conference. It marked the fourth-straight season this team had failed to win a single conference game.

The school had seen enough of Wade Wyatt. His four-year reign—a reign that produced a whopping five victories—was mercifully ended after the lopsided loss to Arkansas.

Wyatt didn't address us after the game. Somebody either told him he was fired or he simply assumed. Either way, Wyatt walked right out of the stadium, got into his big, silver Cadillac, and drove himself back to Texas.

We never saw him again.

Not a tear was shed as news of Wyatt's firing washed through our locker room. In fact, gleeful relief is the feeling that came over me and my teammates when we got word he was gone. We shared high fives and big laughs. Outsiders observing our postgame locker room scene would have thought we were celebrating a victory. They would have had no idea we just embarrassed ourselves with a 55-0 defeat. We didn't care about the loss. We were just glad Coach Wyatt was gone.

But the sense of relief we felt that night didn't last long.

3

"If self-confidence is so important, why would we ever want to approach someone in a manner that might disrupt or shatter it?"

– Pete Carroll, Winner of 2 National Titles and 1 Super Bowl

Weeks went by after Wyatt's firing. The semester ended, I was heading back home for Christmas, and we still didn't have a new head coach.

This wasn't all that surprising. Who would want the job?

Arkansas A&M had been a struggling football program long before Wade Wyatt rolled into town promising to toughen up "this pampered group of slackers," as he put it during his introductory press conference. The Bulldogs hadn't had a winning season since joining the SWC in 1972. There were rumors the other schools in the conference wanted to kick us out of the league for not pulling our weight.

Coach Wyatt was supposed to be the program's savior. He had been a longtime assistant coach in the college ranks. Arkansas A&M was his first (and only) stint as a head coach.

The short-tempered Texan had promised to crack the whip on the Bulldogs. He coached through fear and intimidation. He *loved* to be feared. And we feared him alright. We were terrified of making mistakes. Few were safe from Wyatt's wrath and we did our best to avoid it.

The interesting thing was that the more we feared making mistakes, the more we made them.

In Wyatt's four seasons, Arkansas A&M led the conference in turnovers and penalties each year. Though I don't remember them keeping stats for missed blocks and missed tackles back then, I'm sure we led the conference in those categories as well.

As I paint this unappealing picture of Coach Wade Wyatt, it's fair to question why I signed with Arkansas A&M and agreed to play for a coach like him in the first place.

Two reasons. One, because my high school girlfriend, Sherry, was going to the same college. And two, because it was the only Division 1 school that offered me a scholarship. There wasn't much else to consider.

I was an undersized athlete from a small town in Southeast Kansas, not far from the Arkansas border. I grew up poor. My dad was in and out of jail and my mom was an alcoholic. I don't remember either of them ever holding a job for more than a few months at a time. There was a lot of fear and tension in our house. They were always arguing, fighting, splitting up, and then reuniting.

As a family, we were constantly moving. Tiny rundown houses, trailer parks, cement-walled basement rentals — we lived in all of them. When I got to high school, I spent most of my time crashing with friends.

Looking back now, I understand better the pressures that made my parents the way they were. My dad had grown up thinking he'd graduate high school, get a good-paying job at the local mill, work his forty hours a week and provide a nice, secure living for his family. That's what his father and his father's father had done. That's what the O'Connor men had always done since immigrating from Ireland. There was no need for a college degree.

But by the late 1970s and early 1980s, the job landscape was changing dramatically for blue-collar workers like my dad. I was too young to remember when the textile mill in our little town closed its doors. All I know is that my old man lost a good-paying job and never got back on his feet. He found new jobs here and there, but they never paid anything close to what he made at the mill and the new jobs were never stable. When things got really bad, he'd do something stupid and end up going to jail for a while.

My mom left my dad several times. Sometimes she would take me and my sister with her. Sometimes she wouldn't.

From a young age, I knew something wasn't right with my mom and by the time I was old enough to understand she was escaping from reality with alcohol, it didn't matter much to me — I never really knew her in the first place.

The environment I grew up in didn't look anything like those John Hughes movies my friends and I watched in high school. But I dreamed of a life like that. I dreamed of having a happy family, a nice house, a clean yard — things to be proud of. When I saw people in movies and on TV living those lives, I would daydream about what that must be like. I wanted to have a fun and loving family. I wanted to feel safe and secure. I didn't want to be afraid all the time.

I knew if I wanted to create the type of life I dreamed of, I couldn't follow in my parents' footsteps. I needed to go to college and become the first O'Connor to get a degree. That was the key. But *wanting* to go to college and *affording* to go to college were two very different things.

That's where football came in.

The town I grew up in was one of those football-crazed small towns where everything shut down on Friday nights. That love of the game rubbed off on me at a young age.

When I started playing tackle football in junior high, I realized I was *good* at football. A few of the other parents would pat me on the back after games and tell me how impressed they were. They didn't care who my parents were or how poor I was or where I was living at the moment, they just wanted to tell me how much they admired something I was doing. I can't describe how good that made me feel. I finally had something that made me proud of who I was.

Aside from the positive attention I received, I had *fun* playing football. There was nothing I enjoyed more.

I got obsessed with the game. If I wasn't playing it, I was training for it or watching VHS tapes of old games or recorded shows made by NFL Films and hosted by Steve Sabol.

My parents didn't share my enthusiasm. My dad never attended my games and my mom said my success on the field was making me full of myself. "Here comes Mister Big Shot," she would say. "The kid who thinks he's better than everyone else in this house because he scored a touchdown for his little team in this little town."

Those comments stung. I tried to harness my anger and use it as fuel on the football field. I don't know if that strategy worked or not, but I do know I was able to lose myself on the football field. It was the place where I didn't have to think about anything else. It was my escape from all the tension and fear at home. Football made me happy.

I had an encouraging high school coach and when I was a sophomore, he told me I had the potential to become the best player he'd ever coached. I believed him and gained more confidence each season.

On the football field, I wasn't afraid. I wasn't insecure. I wasn't ashamed of my homelife. On the football field, I was good at something. I was proud of myself. I had fun and experienced joy I rarely felt anywhere else.

My senior year at quarterback, we won the state championship (our town's first) and I made the all-state team. My dream of playing football in college and earning a scholarship seemed like a real possibility. However, I was what most college coaches referred to as, "small-town good." I was considered a risky recruit because even though I had strong stats, I was playing against lower-level high school competition.

As Signing Day neared, it looked like no Division 1 colleges were willing to take a chance on me. I planned on going to a small college or even a junior college. But just three days before Signing Day, Coach Wyatt from Arkansas A&M offered me a full scholarship. I was offered late because his other targeted quarterbacks went elsewhere.

In high school, I was an option quarterback — a run-first QB who relied more on speed, athleticism, and instincts than on reading coverages and passing. Coach Wyatt ran a complicated pro-style offense that liked to keep quarterbacks in the pocket. Arkansas A&M did not seem to be a good fit, but what other choice did I have? I dreamed of playing in a major bowl game like the Cotton Bowl and even though the Bulldogs were the cellar dwellers of the Southwest Conference, maybe things would turn around once I got there.

My girlfriend, Sherry, also decided to go to A&M and that sealed the deal.

Regardless of the unease I had about playing for Wade

Wyatt and whether Arkansas A&M was a good fit for me, I was excited about making my dream come true: playing Division 1 college football. I was proud of myself.

That is, until my parents cut me down to size.

First, it was my dad. He told me, "I don't think you should go to that school. Those guys are on a whole 'nother level. I think you should go somewhere smaller. One of the worst things a man can do is aim higher than he's capable of. It will only lead to embarrassment. I don't want to see that happen to you. You need to be realistic."

Then it was my mother who said to me, "Danny, I see all the attention you're getting. Trust me, it ain't gonna last long. It never does. I bet you don't last two semesters at that school."

The seeds of doubt had been planted and aggressively fertilized.

I never forgot those comments. They would end up being more than just hurtful; they would end up being almost spot-on predictions.

By the time I arrived on the Arkansas A&M campus, the excitement of chasing my dream had fizzled out. From the first day of practice, I knew I had made a mistake coming to this school.

I forced myself to grind through my redshirt season, hoping things would get better. They didn't. Less than a week into my second season, I wanted to quit. Wyatt and the atmosphere he created took the fun out of the sport that had been my escape in high school. I used to look forward to lifting weights, practicing, watching film—anything that had to do with football. Now, I dreaded it all.

Even before my embarrassing performance against Rice, I had made the decision to leave school as soon as the semester was over. I couldn't take it anymore.

We were losing on the field, I was struggling to understand the offense, and I hated being anywhere near Wyatt. Not only because I was afraid of doing something that might attract his fury, but also because he was such a negative guy. His mere presence made me feel bad about myself.

More than a few times standing next to him on the sidelines during a game, I'd watch him call in the play and then say over the headset, "Watch this, I bet these bums can't pick up a single yard." He was almost always proven right.

He constantly told us how awful he thought we were and our performance on the field lived up (or down) to that opinion.

Off the field, things weren't going any better. Sherry broke up with me a few weeks before my infamous performance against Rice. She said I had changed.

"You're so down all the time," she said. "We're in college. We're supposed to be having fun and looking forward to the future, but you see the worst in *everything*. I'm sorry, but I just can't take it anymore."

I tried to defend myself, but she was right. Since coming to this school, I *had* grown grouchier. I was no longer Danny O'Connor, the all-state quarterback and team leader I was back in high school. Now, I was a nameless scout-team QB who my coach wished he'd never recruited in the first place. I responded to my new situation by wallowing in self-pity, making excuses, and becoming that boyfriend who gets jealous because of his own insecurities.

I was also struggling academically. I couldn't find a major I was excited about and my GPA had dropped below 2.0. I was in danger of losing my eligibility to play.

Not that I cared about my eligibility. I wanted out of this place. I wanted to go back to my hometown, move in with one of my old friends, maybe work for a few months, then hit the reset button and figure out what I was going to do with my life.

Maybe my parents were right and I didn't belong in college. Maybe Wyatt was right and I didn't belong on a college football field. Maybe my life had peaked playing football on my small-town high school team. Lord knows the fun I used to have playing the game ended when I stepped on this campus.

If there was any one thing Coach Wyatt and I had in common, it was that we both wished I had never come to Arkansas A&M.

When Wyatt was fired, my joy lasted almost a whole twenty-four hours. I quickly realized that though Wyatt was gone, nothing else had changed. I was still the worst quarterback on the roster and whoever the new coach was would surely see my performance against Rice and urge me to leave the team.

Sherry and I were still broken up. My grades were still in trouble. I still hated the person I had become since arriving on this campus.

I went back home over Christmas break with plans to never come back.

4

"When I come into this clubhouse, if I am dejected and I am depressed and I am tired and my players see me that way, what is the attitude and the atmosphere of the clubhouse going to be? If I walk in full of enthusiasm, full of self-confidence, and proud to be putting that uniform on, all of those things are also contagious. That's the attitude this team will have."

– Tommy Lasorda, 2-Time World Series-Winning Manager

1987

I expected to hear that a new head coach was hired while back home on break. It didn't happen.

I was just curious enough to see who the new head coach would be that I decided I might as well return to campus once the new year started.

Plus, being back home and crashing on friends' couches for a couple weeks made me realize there were some things to be grateful for at college. At least I had a clean dorm room with meals covered by my scholarship. I could hang around campus for a few more weeks, see who the new coach was, and then figure out what to do next.

I was directionless and indecisive — two clear signs of insecurity, I now understand. I had no conviction about where I wanted to go or what I wanted to do next. I didn't want to stay in school, but I also didn't want to leave because I had no plan for what I would do if I left. I was full of angst and unease. I was stuck in a passive state, letting the ever-changing circumstances around me determine my fate. I didn't like who I was or where I was, but I didn't know who I wanted to be or where I wanted to go.

Not helping my anxiety was the fact that two weeks into 1987, with spring-semester classes about to begin, the school *still* had not hired a new coach.

Rumors around campus ranged from the obvious — the school must have swung and missed on several candidates because nobody wanted the job — to the hyperbolic — the school was about to suspend the football program due to its lack of competitiveness.

Talking with teammates, I quickly learned I wasn't the only player who had come back just long enough to see who the new head coach might be — there were several of us with one foot out the door.

We couldn't help but laugh at the situation as each day passed without a new coach. What a joke this team had become. Clearly, no decent coach wanted anything to do with this futile program of ours. We were starting to wonder if those rumors about the football program dying were true. Players were asking, "If we don't have a team, what happens to my scholarship?"

Finally, the day before spring semester classes were set to begin, we got word a press conference would be held to introduce the new head football coach at Arkansas A&M University. Several of us players gathered around the TV in the commons area of our dorm, anxious to find out who our coach would be.

The school's president stood behind the lectern and declared, "It gives me great pleasure to introduce as the next head football coach at Arkansas A&M University: Bud Sullivan."

Who? We all looked at each other, wondering if anyone had heard of this guy.

The TV cameras focused on a fit, young-looking man standing off to the side of the school president. He was smiling a confident, knowing smile — like he was in on a little secret that nobody else knew.

"I never heard of this guy," one of our defensive linemen said. "I thought we'd at least get us a name this time."

My roommate, Brian Dawson, laughed. "I knew we wouldn't get a name. Nobody wants this job."

"Give me a break," another teammate said as he shook his head. "This guy looks like he's still in college. I'm older than this dude!"

As the school president continued his introduction and

tried to convince viewers he had hired "the man who will engineer the turnaround we've all been waiting for," players made jokes about transferring and laughed nervously.

Our new head coach wasn't a famous former player or a seasoned coach. The graphic on the TV stated he was thirty-nine years old, but he looked ten years younger.

When Bud Sullivan took to the lectern and began to speak, we quieted down. He grinned big as he repeated the clichéd statements you would expect to hear at an introductory press conference.

"I'm thrilled to be here."

Just wait, you haven't been here long enough.

"This is a dream job for a guy like me."

You mean a gullible guy? This program is a national laughingstock and you just committed career suicide, pal.

"We're going to be an aggressive football team."

Has any newly-hired coach ever declared he would be bringing in a more passive style of play?

"I believe this program is a sleeping giant."

It ain't sleeping, it's dead.

As I cynically rebutted each of Coach Sullivan's statements in my head, I was struck by how energetic he looked, like he was ready to sprint out of the room and start running practices.

If the administration was looking for someone who embodied the exact opposite of the previous head coach, they had found him in Bud Sullivan.

Coach Wyatt famously wore a giant cowboy hat, he moved slowly and smoked like a chimney, he carried a large gut, he had a perpetual frown, and the deep, dark bags under his eyes made him look desperately in need of a good night's sleep. At press conferences, he answered questions with a bored tone and a gravelly voice that was hard to understand. He seemed irritated by every question he was asked. To everyone he encountered, Wyatt gave off the vibe of an annoyed curmudgeon who just wanted to be left alone.

Coach Sullivan, on the other hand, looked healthy and invigorated. He had a trim, athletic build and a fresh haircut. He couldn't stop smiling. When he said, "I can't wait to get started," I believed him (even if I did think he had no idea what he was getting into). He seemed to enjoy his time in front of the media.

Sullivan cracked jokes throughout the press conference and thoughtfully answered each reporter's questions. He didn't respond with that cranky, condescending, I-can't-believe-I-have-to-waste-my-time-with-such-smallminded-people attitude that some coaches like to give the media. (As someone who is now a member of the sports media, I've come to greatly appreciate coaches and players like Bud Sullivan, people who realize media members are trying to make a living just like they are.)

In short, our new coach seemed young, energetic,

happy, and likable.

For a moment, I was almost excited about the hire. He was so different from Wyatt. I just might *enjoy* playing for this guy.

I caught myself and quickly squelched any hopeful thoughts. *Just wait, Bud Sullivan, this place will grind that enthusiasm right out of you.*

The last two years had created in me a cynical attitude that wouldn't be easy to grow out of.

Two hours later, Bud Sullivan would address our team for the first time.

Though I had no idea then, the day Bud Sullivan was hired would change the path of my life forever.

5

"When you accept the fact that you are in your present condition, good or bad, because of the choices you have made, you will find yourself capable of changing your situation by making better choices."

– Lou Holtz, National Champion Football Coach

The doors in the back of our auditorium-like team meeting room flew open and Bud Sullivan glided towards the small stage in the front of the room. He was chomping gum and though he had an all-business, let's-get-moving demeanor, he also had the same confident smile I noticed at the press conference. He hopped up the stairs of the stage and took his place behind the lectern.

We were all seated at desks in the meeting room. A notebook and pen placed on each desk.

"Listen up everybody, I'm Bud Sullivan and I'm your new head coach. When any coach on this staff is talking, I want you sitting up straight and I want your eyes on us."

The majority of players in the room, including me, had

either been slouching in our chairs or lounging back with stretched-out legs. We repositioned ourselves. We did it slowly, with a few audible sighs throughout the room — we were trying to be cool about it, but we did it nonetheless.

"The notebooks in front of you are yours to keep," Bud continued. "Bring these notebooks to every team meeting you attend and write down the information that is most important. You'll know it when you hear it."

I heard a few more sighs. Though I opened my notebook reluctantly, just like everyone else, I would soon find myself taking notes just as our new head coach had instructed. In fact, to this day, I still have all my old notebooks. They are loaded with a lot more than X's and O's. They contain the greatest lessons Bud would teach me through the years.

"We're gonna have plenty of time to get to know each other over the next several months," Bud said. "But right now, I want to quickly introduce myself and let you know that things are about to change in a big way.

"First off, I want you to know where I'm from. I spent the last five seasons coaching at the University of Oklahoma. I worked with quarterbacks and helped run the offense. Two weeks ago, we beat Arkansas in the Orange Bowl, 42-8, and finished the year ranked number three in the nation. The season before that, we won the National Championship."

Bud talked fast and assertive, with a slight Arkansas accent. He had what you'd call, *good ol' boy swagger.*

Confident and in charge, but still friendly and approachable.

"Before I coached under Barry Switzer at Oklahoma, I coached under Lou Holtz back when he was at Arkansas. For those of you who don't keep up with the rest of the nation, those are two of the top coaches in all of college football. And let me tell you, I learned a lot from those guys.

"The most important thing I learned from them and all the other great coaches I've had the privilege of learning from is this: **Success is a choice. Success is not something that just happens to you, it's something you choose to make happen.**

"You are where you are right now because of the choices you've made. And that means, like it or not, you have chosen to be a last-place football team."

I heard a few uneasy grumbles at that comment. I also found myself writing down exactly what our new coach had just said.

Coach Bud Sullivan smiled at the grumbles and continued unfazed. "I know it's not what you want to hear, but it's the truth. Every single one of you is a result of the choices you've made up to this point. You've chosen to work hard or slack off. You've chosen to go above and beyond or do the bare minimum. You've chosen to lift your teammates up and hold them accountable or put them down because of your own insecurities. You've chosen to attack the day with fearless enthusiasm or cower to your

fears. You've chosen to believe in yourself or tu
You've chosen to raise your expectations of what yu
capable of or lower them to be content with where you are.
These are choices you've made and they've added up to
where you are right now.

"*You* are the culmination of all your choices up to this
point.

"As a team, your record is the culmination of the choices
you have made together. That means you all have made the
choice to be a last-place football team."

More grumbles throughout the room.

"You can get mad at me for saying this if you want to,"
Bud said, "I know you can find all kinds of people and
circumstances to blame for your results. If you go looking
for excuses, you'll have no trouble finding them. That's
what most people do when things don't go their way.
That's how most people justify losing.

"But instead of getting mad at what I'm saying, you
should be getting excited. That's because **if you are where
you are due to the choices you've made in the past, you
can change where you're going by the choices you make
today.** And that's exciting."

He paused to let us write down what he said. I could
sense the attitude of the room shifting just a bit.

"**The single most important choice you can make is
what type of attitude you're going to have**," Bud said.
"*Everything* begins with the attitude you choose. Everything

you do and every thought you think follows your attitude. **Losing follows a losing attitude. Winning follows a winning attitude. It's that simple.**

"If you want to turn things around and start winning, you have to first develop a winning attitude."

6

"A winning culture is built on confidence, love, caring about each other, and looking forward to going to work in the morning."
– Barry Switzer, Winner of 3 National Titles and 1 Super Bowl

Bud had my attention. I felt a spark—just a spark—of something I had not felt in a long time: self-empowerment. The feeling that I might have some control over my destiny after all.

"Barry Switzer taught me that the game of football is played with three components," Bud said.

"First, you've got the physical component. You each have the physical capability of a Division 1 college football player. You wouldn't be here if you didn't. As coaches, it's our job to show you how to maximize that physical capability in the weight room, in practice, and with how you treat your bodies. As players, it's up to you to push yourself harder than you ever have before to reach your maximum physical potential. That's the physical component.

"Second, you've got the mental component of the game. That's knowing what to do and when to do it on the football field. We will master the fundamentals and techniques of this game. We will master our playbooks and assignments. Your coaches will put together scouting reports to ensure you are mentally prepared for every opponent you face. You will be spending lots of time in the film room. That's all part of the mental component of this game.

"The third and final component is psychological. That's your attitude.

"The mental and physical aspects of the game are hugely important. We must master those aspects. We *will* master those aspects.

"However, it's important to understand that every other team across the country is working on the physical and mental. In fact, anyone can master the physical and mental aspects of the game if they are disciplined enough and if they put in enough time and effort.

"Now, if everyone else is working on the physical and mental components, just like we are, where do we find our edge? What is the difference-maker?

"It's the psychological component of the game where teams separate themselves. **It's *attitude* that separates the great teams from everyone else**.

"This goes way beyond football, fellas. In school and in your career after school, it's the same thing. **Anyone can figure out what to do physically and mentally to**

accomplish an objective. But it's your attitude that determines how well you do it. How long you stick with it and how you handle the adversity along the way is determined by your attitude. Your attitude separates you from everyone else.

"I believe everyone in this room is capable of greatness, but it requires the right attitude to unleash that greatness."

Bud paused to let his words sink in. It was also his way of reminding us to write down what he said.

"What does a winning attitude look like?" Bud said. "What is the attitude that turns things around no matter how far down you've fallen?

"It's not complicated. **The key ingredient to a winning attitude is self-confidence. Confident people tend to succeed and insecure people tend to fail.** Simple as that.

"Your self-confidence is determined by how you see yourself—that's your self-image. If you build a confident self-image where you like who you are, you believe in yourself, and you don't worry about what others say or think about you—you're gonna have a lot of success in life. If you have an insecure self-image where you don't like the man you see in the mirror, you doubt yourself, and you worry all the time about what everyone else is saying or thinking about you—well, you're gonna fail in just about everything you do. And you're gonna be a miserable person.

"**Every person lives up to his or her self-confid** ᱐

level. The more you believe in yourself, the more success you will likely have. The more you doubt yourself, the more failure you will likely encounter. That's it. That's the big secret to success.

"**Want to change the results you're experiencing in life? Change the way you see yourself.**

"See yourself as a winner and you'll start acting like a winner, talking like a winner, working like a winner, and treating others like a winner treats others. Do those things and you will *become* a winner. It's only a matter of time."

Bud paused again to make sure we were writing down what he said.

"How you see yourself determines the life you end up living. See yourselves as a championship team and you will eventually become a championship team. See yourselves as a last-place team and that's where you'll stay.

"Confidence means believing in yourself and believing you are destined for success.

"Confidence means *liking* who you are. When you feel good about yourself, good things start happening for you.

"**Great achievers and great teams are full of confidence.** You're not going to be successful in life if you're full of insecurity, self-doubt, and self-pity. You've got to have self-confidence. Lots of self-confidence. You've got to believe you will find a way to achieve your goals. You've got to believe you can get the job done no matter what kind of adversity you're facing.

"And I'm not talking about fake confidence, where people put on a show to hide their insecurities.

"True confidence isn't showy. It's an inner attitude. It's an inner belief about yourself. It's believing in your heart that you have the power to achieve anything you set your mind to. **When your mind believes something can be done, you will find a way to get it done.**"

To my right, I heard a huff and noticed an eye roll from my roommate. Like me, Brian had just completed his redshirt freshman season. Unlike me, Brian was probably the most naturally-talented player on our team.

Though Brian slacked off a lot, when he went all-out, he was a human wrecking ball. He was built like a tank and had amazing speed for a guy his size — a prototypical 1980s middle linebacker. But Brian was also a bit of a clown and often blew off the coaches. He was one of the few players who didn't fear the previous coaching staff because he knew they couldn't afford to lose him. He had the talent to start as a true freshman, but he was redshirted — the coaches hoped he would grow up. While he grew in size and speed during his redshirt year, he didn't grow in maturity.

The previous season (1986), as a starter, Brian had forgettable games where his head wasn't in it. But he also had four games with double-digit tackles. It was during those games where Brian stood high above everyone else on the roster — the one bright spot on our team. He was even named to the Southwest Conference's All-Freshman team.

Joline was Brian's hometown and he often reminded me and anyone else within earshot that the only reason he came to Arkansas A&M was because his dad made him. (His dad had played here and now worked for the university.)

Like everyone else on the roster, Brian Dawson didn't want to be on this team. Unlike just about everyone on the roster, Brian had the talent to play anywhere else in the country.

"Here's the great thing about confidence," Bud said with a big grin. "Not only will confidence lead you to more success, but it will also allow you to have more fun in life. I look at you all and I see a group of young men who haven't had a lot of *fun* lately. That's gonna change. We're gonna win a lot of football games and we're gonna have a helluva lot of fun doing it."

Football and *fun*. Two words I had not heard used together since arriving on this campus.

Coach Wyatt never talked about *fun*. He talked about mistakes and the severe punishments that awaited those who made them. He talked about how pathetic we were and how embarrassed we should feel about ourselves.

"Football is the greatest sport ever invented," Bud said. "Yes, it's rough and tough and it requires blood, sweat, and tears. But you know that? That's fun! It's fun to run somebody over. It's fun to break tackles, outrun the other guy, and score touchdowns. It's fun to take your opponent's very best shot, to get back up and tell him, 'I'm still standing here, I'm not going anywhere.' That's fun, isn't it?"

I nodded in response and realized, for the first time in a long time, I was starting to smile at the thought of playing football.

And I wasn't the only one. I noticed several other nods and smiles throughout the room.

"I want you guys to love coming to work each day," Bud said. "I want you to be passionate about playing this wonderful game. I want you to be full of enthusiasm every single day.

"Football is a tough sport. Nobody will ever deny that. But it's still a game and games are supposed to be fun.

"If you choose to see working out and playing ball as a grind, then that's what you'll experience. If you choose to see it as a game, *that's* what you'll experience. Choose to see it as the game you fell in love with when you were a kid. Choose to be excited about playing this great game of ours.

"Fellas, we're going to turn this thing around. And I don't mean eking out a few wins each season. Everyone in this room is going to be part of one of the greatest turnarounds in college football history.

"The turnaround starts with confidence. I want you to believe in yourselves and I want you to have fun while you're here! This time in your life goes by so fast and I want you to enjoy it."

Bud stopped to read the room. He looked over his team from right to left, and his face turned serious.

"Today is a fresh new start for every person in this room," he said. "That should be exciting to you. What you did or didn't do in the past is over. It's gone. Every single one of you has a clean slate. What you do from this point forward is all that matters. Our record as a team is zero-and-zero and your record as a player is the same. Today is a new day and all I care about is what you do next. You don't get many opportunities like this in life. Take advantage of it.

"Starting today, you've got a lot of very important choices to make. The first and most important choice you need to make is what type of attitude you're going to have. Are you going to be confident or insecure? Are you going to be positive or negative? Excited or apathetic? Are you going to have a winner's attitude or a loser's? Fellas, it really is your choice."

Bud then announced that our first team workout would be the next morning and he exited right.

As soon as Bud left the stage, I saw a few guys nodding, liking what they heard. I saw some wide eyes. I heard one of my teammates say, "Okay, okay, I kinda' like this guy." Most the team appeared to be approving of our new coach's message.

But I also saw a few of our seniors-to-be sharing a laugh with each other. I couldn't hear what they were saying, but the give-me-a-break nature of their body language was obvious.

Brian smacked me on the shoulder. "Could they have

hired a cheesier coach than this guy?"

I shrugged, trying to be cool. "I didn't think he was that bad."

"Don't tell me you're falling for all this rah-rah stuff? That ain't gonna work here. Oklahoma is Oklahoma because of their talent. It's got nothing to do with attitude and confidence. Shoot, if we had Oklahoma's talent, we'd be confident and having fun too. You know why? Because we'd be *winning*. This Bud Sullivan guy is full of crap and his schtick is gonna get real old real quick. You watch."

It was going to take a lot more than one motivational speech to change the cynical culture that had permeated this program for years.

7

"It all boils down to choices. We all have one life to live, so we need to look in the mirror and ask, 'How do I want to be remembered?'"

– Gary Carter, 11-Time MLB All-Star and Baseball Hall of Famer

A few hours after our introductory team meeting with Bud Sullivan, I made a run to the campus bookstore to buy the books I would need for the semester ahead.

I decided I would give this new coach a try. What did I have to lose?

With the gifts of years and maturity, I look back now and wonder why I even struggled with the decision. Clearly, it was my own insecurity and a healthy dose of self-pity urging me to quit school. I envisioned heading back home with a ready-made excuse for why my college career fizzled out: me and the new coach just didn't click. It was an opportunity to save face with my old friends.

But it wouldn't be true.

Based on my introduction to Bud and despite Brian's

skepticism after that first team meeting, the new coach seemed like someone I just might enjoy playing for.

Here was a guy talking about a fresh new start, something I was desperately seeking, but didn't expect to find at Arkansas A&M. He was talking about having fun and enjoying the college experience — a concept completely foreign to the previous coaching staff. He was talking about building up our confidence so we could push ourselves to new heights — not breaking us down to the point we didn't like ourselves.

I figured going through spring ball would at least give me an idea of whether Bud was serious about creating the environment he talked about creating.

Plus, all through the afternoon after that initial meeting with Bud, I couldn't stop asking myself, *What if Bud Sullivan is right?*

What if success *is* a choice? What if my own insecurity was causing me to play poorly on the football field, perform poorly in the classroom, and act like a jealous jerk around my girlfriend (*ex*-girlfriend, that is)? What if I only had myself to blame, no one else?

What if Bud Sullivan is right?

What if it *was* possible to change my life by changing my attitude?

This wasn't the first time I had heard about the importance of attitude. This was the '80s, after all — a time when upbeat thinking and the power of your mindset was seared into the culture. It was a message reinforced by many popular songs and movies of the time.

But just because they said it in movies and sang about it in songs didn't mean everyone was buying into it. Like a lot of guys on this team, I came from a poor family. It was borderline insulting to think my family and people like them could have had a better life if only they had chosen a better attitude. Those ideas may have sold books and concert tickets, but they weren't realistic.

And if I was on the fence regarding the issue prior to college, my time at Arkansas A&M had given me a hard shove in the direction of pessimism. All the losing I experienced — on and off the field — made me see myself as a victim of luck or fate or injustice or some combination of all three. I had unluckily picked the wrong school, the wrong girlfriend, and the wrong classes. Nobody in my family graduated from college, why should I expect my destiny to be any different? I was a victim of my circumstances. Nothing was my fault.

But...*what if Bud Sullivan is right?*

What if I could change my destiny by changing my attitude?

And who was I kidding? If I went back home, I'd never go to another college. I'd follow the path of my parents, hopping from one unfulfilling job to the next while collecting unemployment checks in-between. Was that the life I wanted? Was that the cycle I wanted to continue?

What if Bud Sullivan is right?

What if today is the fresh new start I've been waiting for? What if my future is up to me? What if I really am in control of my destiny?

I may not have been completely convinced Bud was right, but I realized there wasn't much to lose if he was wrong. I didn't like feeling bad about myself. I didn't like being insecure. I wanted to be confident and to feel good about myself. And here was a coach promising to help me do exactly that. Why not give him a try? Why did I have to lose?

What if Bud Sullivan is right?

My nineteen-year-old self may have been insecure and cynical, but I was at least smart enough to realize sticking around was better than the alternative.

I was going to give this Bud Sullivan guy a chance.

8

"Hard work without enthusiasm leads to tedium. Enthusiasm without industriousness leads to unrealized potential. When combined, they cement a solid foundation."

– John Wooden, 10-Time National Champion Basketball Coach

We got our first taste of what it would be like playing for the new coaching staff during winter workouts. How would all this talk of *having fun* translate to the weight room and running sprints until you dropped? What would *confidence* and *enthusiasm* look like during a grueling conditioning session?

Coach Wyatt never talked about things like *confidence*. He certainly never said anything about having *fun*. His motivational tool was fear and that fear-based approach carried over to the weight room.

Seniors and starters were encouraged to haze underclassmen into shape. This made for a tense environment in the weight room. I was always looking over my shoulder. I saw enough teammates get ridiculed for failing a rep that I made sure not to push myself too hard. I didn't want to miss a rep and pay the humiliating price.

I wasn't the only one who adopted this approach. None of us wanted to work too hard and fail because that failure would make us a target. It was like trying to avoid that bully at recess in elementary school — you kept your head down and tried to go by unnoticed.

But things were about to change.

Bud Sullivan gathered us around prior to our first training session of the new era.

"Before we get started," Bud said, "I want to make a few things clear. Everything I talked about yesterday — confidence, enthusiasm, attitude — it all applies to the way you train just as much as it applies to the way you play, the way you study, and the way you carry yourselves. Everything you do is powered by your attitude.

"I want *enthusiasm* in here. I want this weight room to be a high-energy place. We're going to have loud music playing and we're going to keep the energy level up during every workout.

"I want nothing but positive energy in here. Hazing, slacking off, making fun of someone who is giving it everything he's got, none of that will be tolerated. We're not going to let negative energy into this weight room. We're going to encourage each other at all times. This is going to be a positive environment.

"I want you to look forward to coming to work each day

because I know **you will work harder at something you enjoy doing than at something you dread doing**. We're going to work harder than ever before and we're going to enjoy the process of getting stronger, faster, and better in every way possible.

"Don't dread coming to work in the morning. Don't complain about it. Don't get frustrated by it. Get excited about it! Hard work should be *fun*!

"I know what some of you are thinking. What about when you're in pain and you're sore and tired and hurting and you just want to go home and rest? What's fun about that?

"Well, doing something easy isn't fun; it's boring. It's no fun to be stagnant; it's fun to grow. **It's no fun to have something handed to you; it's fun when you go out and earn it.** It's exciting to do hard things and break through barriers.

"When you're tired and hurting, focus on what you're earning by pushing yourself through the pain: a stronger body, a stronger mind, and victories in the fall. Choose to focus on the positive even in the pain.

"You should walk into this gym every day excited to see how you're going to improve yourself. Every single rep makes you stronger, faster, and more confident. Hard work builds your body, your mind, and your soul. If that's not exciting, I don't know what is."

I saw some nods and heard a few claps. Bud's energy

was pumping up some of the troops.

"By working harder than you ever have before, you will not only get physically stronger, you will also get mentally stronger. **Hard work builds confidence faster than anything else I know. The harder you work, the more confident you will become.**"

Bud paused to let his point linger.

"When I was at Oklahoma, we won a lot of games before they even started," Bud said. "Seriously, as soon as we took the field you could just sense the other team didn't have a chance. We had a level of confidence our opponents couldn't come close to. You could see the confidence in our eyes—that inner *knowing* that we were gonna win this game. Other teams tried to fake it, we actually had it.

"**Almost every single time two teams take the field, the more confident team ends up winning**. And that's true off the field as well. The more confident guy gets the job, lands the sale, and wins over the client. He's the guy everyone looks to for help when things are going wrong. **Confidence is the hallmark of a winner.**

"To be confident, you can't be afraid to fail. **It may sound strange, but failure *builds* confidence if it's used properly.**

"If you're not pushing yourself to failure, you'll never take the next step forward. Pushing yourself so hard that you can't finish that last rep is not something to be embarrassed about—it means you're pushing your muscles harder than they've ever been pushed before and they will get stronger because of it. Missing a rep is something to be proud of because it proves you gave it everything you possibly could.

"I want you to check your ego at the door and *fail* your way to more confidence. I want you to do extremely hard things and realize, 'I'm still standing here. What didn't kill me made me stronger.' That's how you build confidence.

"When you push yourself as hard as you can, you *will* backtrack at times. That's to be expected. Progress isn't a straight line. It often requires one step back before you can take two steps forward. But the failure today is how you break through to success tomorrow.

"That's what it means to fail forward. You have to break yourself down before you can build yourself up. When you push yourself to the max and come up short, don't hang your head. You should do just the opposite. Hold your head high when you walk out of here because the step back today will lead to a step forward tomorrow. You may not feel like it when it happens, but by hitting your breaking point, you made yourself stronger — physically, mentally, and spiritually.

"When you can walk out of here knowing you gave it every last bit of energy you have, you should feel good about yourself regardless of what the results were that day."

Bud then looked over the room and gave us a smile.

"There are two things you always control." He held up two fingers. "Your effort and your attitude. The two are intertwined. **Better effort leads to a better attitude and a better attitude fuels better effort. It's a self-perpetuating cycle.**

"That's why the harder you work, the more confident you will get. And the more confident you get, the harder you will work. This work-to-confidence cycle makes you virtually unstoppable.

"**Want to be more confident? Decide to be the hardest worker in the room.** If everyone has that attitude, we'll become the hardest-working team in the conference. By becoming the hardest-working team, we will become the most confident team. And that, fellas, is an awesome advantage over everyone else. That will make us the best team in the conference."

Several guys hollered their approval. None of us had heard things put this way before and we liked what we were hearing.

"And here's the exciting thing," Bud said. "When you make the choice to give your very best effort every day in the weight room, it becomes a habit. And that habit carries over to everything else you do. It carries over to the way you practice in the spring, the summer, and in the fall. It carries over to the way you play on gameday. It carries over to the way you study in school. It carries over to the way you treat others.

"The habit of giving nothing less than your very best begins right now. You can't let up an inch.

"The hard work we do in the weight room is preparing your body for battle on the football field. **The better prepared you are, the more confident you will be.**

"Those who doubt themselves know they haven't prepared properly. The guy who knows he's put in his very best effort to be prepared mentally and physically approaches gameday with confidence. The guy who knows he's put in the long hours studying walks into test day confident he will ace that test.

"**If you want to be more confident, decide to work harder and be more prepared. It really is that simple.**

"What you do in this weight room sets the tone for everything else. Victories don't just happen on Saturday afternoons. They are made today. Let's win this day!"

I heard someone shout, "Let's get after it, boys."

"One last thing I want you to remember whenever you step foot in this weight room," Bud said. "To paraphrase the founder of the Chicago Bears, George Halas, **nobody ever regretted giving their best**.

"Remember that. Give your best every single day and I promise you'll have no regrets."

Bud then introduced us to our new strength and conditioning coach.

The speech Bud gave us that day established how we were expected to train, practice, and carry ourselves for the entirety of our time in the program.

It also set a standard for how we should approach life after our playing days. It's a standard I've tried to remind myself of every day since.

Nobody ever regretted giving their best.

9

"Confidence is the result of hours and days and weeks and years of constant work and dedication."

– Roger Staubach, Heisman Trophy Winner & Super Bowl MVP

It's been said that the most important assistant coach on a coaching staff is the strength and conditioning coach. This is because he spends more time with the players than any other coach.

Our new S&C coach was a guy named Marty Stonebreaker and he bought in fully to Bud Sullivan's coaching philosophy. With a broad chest and ripcord arms, Stonebreaker was in his late twenties and looked more like a player than a coach. He was loud and enthusiastic. He bounced around the weight room and would often jump into one of our workouts and bang out some reps as he encouraged us.

This was much different from our previous S&C coach, a slow-moving guy who spent most of his time in the back office after posting a printout of the weekly workout on the bulletin board.

Stonebreaker never stopped moving and his energy was infectious. He was loud but encouraging, repeating his favorite phrases often:

"How great is this?"

"Attack this day with joy and enthusiasm!"

"Nobody is gonna outwork us! *Nobody!*"

I would soon realize that every coach on Bud's staff shared his philosophy. No one was quite as energetic as Coach Stonebreaker, but each coach preached a message of confidence and thinking like a winner. They stressed the importance of taking care of each other and bringing an enthusiastic attitude to the team.

The coaches wanted high-energy players. Going through the motions was not an option. Starting with Stonebreaker in the weight room, all the coaches kept an eye out for what they called, "half-assing reps." If you weren't giving your best, they called you on it. From the starters to the scout team, nobody was allowed to slack off.

Those first winter workouts with the new staff clarified that Bud Sullivan's message of confidence, enthusiasm, and fun didn't mean life as a football player at Arkansas A&M was going to be easy. *Fun* and *easy* were not the same thing.

Bud's brand of positive thinking wasn't: think happy thoughts, coast along, and all your desires will be given to you.

Far from it.

Bud's idea of positivity required hard work.

Extremely hard work.

In fact, I never worked so hard in my life.

Over the next few months, each workout built on the last one. We were "raising the bar just a little bit every day," Stonebreaker liked to remind us. We did a lot more maxing-out on reps and this new style of training wasn't appreciated by some members of the team.

"If the coaches keep this up, they're not gonna have any players left," Brian said after one particularly-grueling workout.

With the previous staff, we learned that if you kept your mouth shut and did what you were told, regardless of how hard you did it, you could skate through workouts and practices without attracting unwanted attention. If you tried too hard, you might mess up and nobody wanted that. It was better to coast along, do what you were told, and do the bare minimum.

Things were different now.

Failing to hit your last rep was no longer something to be punished for (proof you were weak), it was something you were congratulated for (proof you were pushing yourself as hard as you could). Losing your lunch on that final sprint was no longer something to be ridiculed for (proof you were out of shape), it was something to be commended for (proof you were emptying your tank and giving everything you had).

And Bud was right. The harder I worked, the better I felt about myself.

There were days when I was so sore from a squat session, I couldn't get out of bed without wincing in pain. But the pain felt *good*. The soreness was a badge of honor, a reminder that I had pushed myself to a new level.

Some days I left the weight room frustrated after failing on my last rep, failing to hit a new max. But I reminded myself I was failing forward. Today's breakdown would lead to stronger muscles tomorrow. Sure enough, a week or two later I would be back on track, hitting new maxes.

And with each new max or faster time on a conditioning drill, I felt better about the body I was building. I walked just a little taller throughout the day.

For the first time since coming to Arkansas A&M, I was starting to like who I saw when I looked in the mirror. And it was all because of how hard I was working.

The harder you work, the better you feel about yourself. This is one of those lessons I've seen play out my entire life. I'm not talking about drudgery, of course. I'm not talking about working for work's sake at something you can't stand doing. I'm talking about those moments in life when you feel like everything is going wrong and your natural inclination is to freeze up and hope the problems go away. That never works. It only leads to more anxiety and stress.

Instead, I've noticed that whenever I find myself on a

losing streak of some kind, the most effective thing I can do is start working on something that is important to me. It could be something career related, it could be a hobby, or it could be an exhausting workout at the gym. Whatever it may be, I find that taking action and working hard at something I enjoy is one of the quickest cures for worry and stress in any situation.

Hard work is good for the soul. But unfortunately, not everyone understands this. That was certainly the case for our team at Arkansas A&M.

Though a lot of guys were feeling more confident and buying into Bud's message the way I was starting to, Brian's prediction was correct. The intense workouts *were* taking their toll on some players and the roster continued to thin out.

We ended up losing a total of fourteen players during the first few months of the Bud Sullivan era. We had never been pushed this hard and it was pushing some guys right out the door.

As Coach Stonebreaker said one afternoon, "**Hard work isn't for everybody. Neither is winning.**"

10

"Arrogance requires advertising. Confidence speaks for itself."

– Mike Krzyzewski, 5-Time National Champion Basketball Coach

After becoming our head coach, Bud began holding mandatory Sunday night meetings in the winter and spring. Every Sunday we would all meet for two hours in the team meeting room. These Sunday night meetings were focused on the psychological component of the game—things like confidence, attitude, goal-setting, and so on. My old notebooks are full of the notes I took at these meetings and I still refer to them. Through the years, several of my teammates and I have happily reminisced about how much we learned from Bud's Sunday night meetings.

One Sunday in the winter of '87, Bud made a point about confidence I never forgot.

"We're making progress this offseason," he said. "I see the intensity and the energy in the weight room. I see the lifts going up and the forty times coming down. I look around and I see a few of you guys with that look in your eye, that look that says, 'I'm gonna do something great; I'm gonna be someone special.' That look is unmistakable and I love seeing it.

"I'm also watching how you all carry yourselves—in these facilities and walking around campus. Some of you are walking taller. Some of you are giving off that confident vibe that you must have if you want to be successful. Again, I love seeing that.

"But I'm also seeing something troubling from some of you. I'm watching some guys try to fake confidence. You're trying hard to act confident, but it's all a show.

"Here's something everyone needs to understand: **you can't fake confidence. In fact, fake confidence is worse than no confidence.**

"Fake confidence is the guy who is hiding his own insecurity by trying to look mean all the time. He's quick to put others down. He thinks if he acts tough or indifferent or demeaning, he'll seem confident. That's not confidence.

"Fake confidence is also the guy who acts arrogant and obnoxious. He tries to hide his insecurity by being loud and disrespectful to everyone. He thinks if he acts like he doesn't care, he'll seem confident.

"Both those guys are examples of fake confidence. They're trying to get attention and seem important, but everybody can see right through them. They're trying to hide their own insecurities. They're doing the very things that actually *hurt* their self-confidence.

"When I was a young assistant coach at Arkansas, Lou Holtz told me, '**You want to build self-confidence? Follow these three rules:**

"'**One, always do the right thing.**

"'**Two, do everything to the very best of your ability.**

"'**Three, genuinely care about other people.**'

"What an eye-opening lesson that was for me. Coach Holtz made the point that by following those three rules you will feel good about yourself. When you feel good about yourself, you become more confident.

"You all know what it means to do the right thing. Don't lie. Don't cheat. Don't steal. Treat everyone with respect, the way you would like to be treated. Be kind to others.

"**How you treat others reveals your own self-image.** If you're disrespectful to others or act like you don't care about them, it reveals that you don't have much respect for yourself. If you put others down, it shows exactly what you think of yourself.

"The insecure guy lives in fear and he tries like hell to hide that fear by acting tough and stoic or obnoxious and loud. He's so worried about what other people think of him that he's always putting on a show.

"**The genuinely confident man treats others with respect. He does the right thing regardless of what anyone else might say or think.**

"Confidence isn't a show, it's an inner belief, something deep down inside that says, 'I am proud of who I am. There is no obstacle too big for me. Bring it on, I can do it!'

"**No matter what the challenge, the confident man doesn't pretend he can succeed; he *knows* he can succeed. He doesn't do something because of how it might look to others; he does something because he knows it's the right thing to do. Period.**

"Building this type of self-confidence isn't easy. We live in a world full of self-conscious people who are always trying to impress or one-up somebody else. Genuine self-confidence requires mental toughness to shut out the opinions of naysayers and bad influences. It requires discipline and integrity to not take the easy way out when the right thing to do is the harder thing to do.

"Every one of you needs more confidence. Not arrogance; confidence. And **confidence is directly linked to how you carry yourself and how you treat others**.

"How you treat others not only reveals your inner confidence, it can also *build* your inner confidence.

"When you treat others the right way — the way you would like to be treated — it makes you feel good about yourself. When you make others feel good about themselves, it comes right back to you.

"Feeling good about yourself is positive fuel for your self-image. Be kind to others. Be respectful. Look people in the eye and smile. I'm telling you, it goes a long way towards building up your confidence.

"Don't be the insecure guy who is afraid to smile and

say 'hi' to somebody because you're afraid they won't return the favor. Be the confident guy who is going to smile and say 'hi' regardless of whether it's returned. The confident person does the right thing and doesn't take it personally if someone else doesn't appreciate it.

"Taking the high road is another sign of strength and confidence. When you're secure in yourself, even people antagonizing you won't bother you all that much. You'll be able to laugh off insults and critics. That's confidence. Insecure people are touchy and easily offended — don't let that be you.

"Your self-image has serious consequences in every area of your life. I hope you all understand this. Treat others with respect. Do the right thing. Carry yourself with pride and dignity. That's what real confidence is. Don't try to fake it."

This was another one of those lessons that had a lasting impact on me.

After college, I pursued a career in sports radio and I reminded myself often of Bud's words about treating people with respect and doing the right thing. As I worked my way up in the business and landed my own sports talk show, I decided early on that I would not be the guy who made his mark slamming athletes and coaches. I saw other personalities in the business gain lots of fame and fortune for doing exactly that. They were always ripping sports figures, airing salacious rumors about them, and spending their shows poking fun at the mistakes others made.

I didn't want to be that guy. It's one thing to second-guess play-calls and debate strategies; it's quite another to demean people and take personal shots at them. I reminded myself to treat others the way I wanted to be treated. If that meant I would not become as rich and famous as other sports talk hosts, so be it.

Through the years, I ended up gaining a large audience that seemed to appreciate my style of sports talk. I'm glad to say that while those of us who share this philosophy may not make as many headlines as some of our "shock jock" competitors, we've been able to have careers we love while still feeling good about ourselves at the end of the day.

Bud was right. You gain confidence when you do the right thing. And you sleep a lot better, too.

11

"What you fear is what you create. ... If you have confidence, you will perform at the level you aspire to. If you have fear, you will never achieve that level."

– Augie Garrido, 5-Time National Champion Baseball Coach

Spring ball introduced us to what life on the football field would look like with Bud Sullivan in charge.

The spring football season consists of four weeks of practice, which culminates in an intra-squad scrimmage. Though spring ball is less intense than the summer practices that precede the regular season, it's still an important time to prove yourself and compete for a better spot on the depth chart.

Right away, it was obvious things were going to be much different with the new coaching staff.

When Wade Wyatt was our coach, he would walk slowly and observe from a distance while practice was going on, waiting for someone to mess up. He was like a schoolyard bully looking over a pool of potential victims. I went through practices tight and nervous, feeling his glare on my shoulders, always hoping I wouldn't do something that would cause him to yell at me.

"O'Connor, what the hell was that?!" he yelled at me a handful of times over the past two seasons.

He would then say to my position coach, "Frank, clean it up or you'll be looking for a new job."

"Yes, sir," my position coach would yell back to his dictator. The coaches were just as petrified of Wyatt's wrath as the players were. If you got called out as a player, your position coach would get called out and then he'd take it out on you—an ugly cycle of fearful repercussions.

Every so often, Wyatt would stomp towards a player who had irked him by fumbling the ball, dropping a pass, missing a blocking assignment, something like that (things that happened often, but Wyatt would suddenly decide he'd seen enough). He'd grab the player by his facemask and swing him this way and that—cussing him up and down through red-faced fury.

These thrashings were always followed by some type of punishment, usually pushups that included a few demeaning kicks to the backside as the player dropped to the ground. Often times, the punishment would be running stairs up and down the nearby bleachers.

A dozen or so times throughout the season, Wyatt would get so mad he'd stop practice and make everyone run gassers (sprints down and back across the fifty-yard width of the field) until we started dropping.

Looking back, I never understood why Wyatt thought it was a good idea to waste so much time meting out punishments when that time could have been spent practicing the very techniques that would alleviate the mistakes he was so upset about.

Three times during my two seasons with Wyatt, he stopped practice and made his coaching staff run gassers. I never understood this either. How were we supposed to respect our coaches after seeing them demeaned in front of us like that?

The result was that we all played in fear of making a mistake. I was constantly worried about making bad reads, fumbling the ball, or throwing a pick. Mistakes were all I thought about.

Enter Bud Sullivan and the new way of doing things at Arkansas A&M.

As soon as our first spring practice started and I saw our new head coach grinning big as he ran onto the field, I knew things were going to be different.

"What a perfect day for football," he said as he reached us at midfield. "It's a great day to be a Bulldog!"

Bud started every single practice with those two lines. It didn't matter if it was bright and sunny, hot and humid, or if an icy rain was pouring down on him. He said it every time. And he meant it.

The positive tone to start things off was just one of many

changes.

Bud didn't spend practice striking fear into his assistant coaches. He let his position coaches coach their positions.

As players walked to the practice field or went through stretches and warmups at the start of practice, Bud would walk around and greet us, asking questions about how we were feeling, how school was going, how our parents were doing, things like that. He liked to joke around with us and get us laughing. Many times, he reminded us to enjoy playing football and being college kids.

It wasn't uncommon for Bud to walk up to a straight-faced player and say, "I want to see you smile. You work harder when you enjoy what you're doing and what's not to love about getting to play football today?"

Bud was also the team's offensive coordinator and play caller, so he spent most of practice working with the quarterbacks and running backs who would make up his new wishbone backfield. As a quarterback, I spent a lot of time with him, learning the triple-option offense he was installing.

To be clear, the upbeat vibe I'm describing was not lackadaisical or undisciplined. Once the stretching and warm-ups were done, practice was intense. The fundamentals of the game and highly-detailed football techniques—things many of us had taken for granted over the years—were stressed repeatedly. Everything from the exact finger placement he wanted quarterbacks like me to grip the football with to a lineman's foot being moved just a few degrees outward to a cornerback's precise hand position when lining up in tight coverage — I saw it all stressed like never before. There was a right way to do things and this was hammered home.

I should also point out that while mistakes were handled differently, they were not tolerated. I heard Bud say on several occasions, "Victory favors the team that makes the fewest mistakes." But he would always follow that up with, "Preparation and repetition will eliminate mistakes."

Instead of putting the fear of God in us about what would happen if we made a mistake, Bud was instilling within us the confidence that we would be less likely to make a mistake due to our preparation.

Mistakes are inevitable, of course, and when they were made, Bud or an assistant coach would quickly step in and show us the corrections they wanted made. Sometimes the mistake was mental, often it was technical. Either way, it was addressed constructively.

The best way to describe this new atmosphere is to say the coaches were demanding, but not demeaning. We were no longer ridiculed for errors. Bud and his staff focused on teaching us how to avoid those errors in the future.

They taught everything from a positive perspective. That is, they'd stress what they *wanted* us to do, not what they *didn't* want us to do.

Bud would tell me, "Hold onto the ball tight, like this."

And then he'd demonstrate exactly where he wanted my hands on the ball. Never once did I hear him say, "Don't fumble the ball." During passing drills, he never said, "You better not throw an interception." Instead, he'd say, "See your target clearly and step in with confidence when throwing the ball." And then he'd show me the exact passing mechanics he wanted me to use.

These may have been subtle differences, but I look back now and see what Bud was doing. It was smart psychology. He didn't want to use negative language. He didn't want to put the vision of failure into our minds. Instead, he wanted us to envision success.

Bud wanted me to see myself throwing a perfect pass, not throwing an interception. He wanted me to focus on making the right option read, not the fear of making the wrong read. He wanted my thoughts on powering through a tackler with a tight grip on the ball, not fumbling.

"**Focus on what you want to happen, not what you don't**," Bud would say. "**What you focus on most tends to come about.**"

Over the three years I played for Bud, I heard him repeat those two phrases dozens of times.

"**If you focus on what you want to achieve, you're more likely to experience achievement**," he said. "**If you focus on what you fear, you're more likely to experience the very thing you fear.**"

As practices went on I realized I was thinking less about

making mistakes and more about making great plays. I started to actually have *fun* on the football field again.

However, old habits die hard and despite feeling freer and more confident *at times*, I still played mostly tight and fearful. I had humiliated myself so badly the previous season that I couldn't let go of my past mistakes. I couldn't stop replaying them in my head.

Luckily, Bud had a solution.

12

"What to do with a mistake: recognize it, admit it, learn from it, forget it."

– Dean Smith, 2-Time National Champion Basketball Coach

Coming from Oklahoma, Bud Sullivan brought with him the wishbone offense — a high-powered rushing attack that had led the Sooners to three national titles. The wishbone was a triple-option offense that favored quarterbacks with speed and athleticism over pure passing ability. It was similar to the split-back veer offense I had run in high school and I knew it would play to my talents more than the other quarterbacks on our roster — QBs who were slower on their feet, but better passers. It wasn't outlandish to think I might be the best fit out of all our quarterbacks for Bud's offense.

However, as spring ball came and went, I realized I wouldn't be competing for the starting job anytime soon. And that was just fine with me. Truthfully, I didn't *want* the starting job. I was so embarrassed by the mistakes I made in the past that I figured it wouldn't be so bad to spend the next three years on the sidelines and out of the spotlight. With Bud as the coach, practices were more enjoyable. Why not simply lay low and enjoy my time here without risking another humiliating moment like I had experienced in the past?

That's how insecure and afraid I was. I would rather ride the bench for three years than risk failing again.

During the spring game, the intra-squad scrimmage on the last day of spring ball, I didn't see action until the second half. I completed two-of-five passes for twenty-four yards and ran the ball eight times for forty-six yards. No scores myself, but we did score touchdowns on two option plays where I made the correct reads before pitching the ball to my halfback.

But those weren't the only statistics of note.

The most memorable stats about my spring-game performance were my two fumbles and one interception. My propensity to turn the ball over had not magically disappeared when the new staff arrived.

When spring ball wrapped up, I was third on the depth chart despite being faster than the number one and number two quarterbacks. Jerry Miller was the starter for most of the last season and looked likely to be the starter as a senior in '87. Mike Pederson held onto the number two spot. He was the guy who burned his redshirt as a true freshman when he came in for me during the Rice game, which meant he would be a sophomore in terms of eligibility (just like me) heading into the season.

Jerry and Mike were both better equipped for a pro-style offense. They were tall guys with strong arms, but heavy feet. Though my skillset was better suited for Bud's option offense, Jerry and Mike both protected the ball better. And, frankly, they both wanted to be starters more than I did.

Bud used the weeks heading into summer to conduct one-on-one meetings with everyone on the team. Some guys came out of these meetings with new positions.

When it was my turn, I entered Bud's office curious to see where I stood with the new coach.

"Hey Danny, great to see you," Bud said as he motioned for me to have a seat across from his desk.

I reminded myself to sit up straight.

"I'm gonna cut right to the chase," he said. "You're the most athletic quarterback we've got and we could use your talent in our backfield. The problem is, I watch you play and I see a guy who is sometimes great with the ball, but other times timid and indecisive. I see a guy who plays in fear. We can't have that, especially at quarterback.

"So, what's the problem? What's got you playing with so much fear?"

This was not how I envisioned my first one-on-one meeting with Bud. I thought if he didn't ask me to change positions or schools, he'd treat me as if everything was going along as planned. That is, something along the lines of, 'You're doing a good job as a back-up, keep your head up and be ready because you never know when we might need you, sport.' Instead, Bud wanted to know why I wasn't moving up the depth chart more than I did.

"I wish I knew," I said, not being honest.

Bud gave me a skeptical look as he leaned back in his desk chair. "I watched that Rice game." He said it almost like he was asking a question, wanting me to respond.

I lowered my eyes as my stomach turned queasy. I knew Bud had surely watched the film from last year's games, but there was a part of me that hoped the Rice game footage had been lost forever. Every time I thought of that game, humiliation enveloped me.

I wanted to shrink away.

"Not my finest moment," I said, trying to make light of it and hide the intense embarrassment I felt.

"That was a tough one. No doubt about it. But you're still here. You didn't quit. You didn't run away and bury your head in shame. That says something to me."

I looked back up at Bud. This was the first time anybody had managed to find a *positive* about the way I handled my disastrous performance.

"Thanks, Coach," I said.

"Do you want to keep playing quarterback?"

"I'll play wherever you want me to," I said, the standard line most players respond with when a coach asks them what position they want to play.

Again, I wasn't being completely honest. (**It's interesting how insecurity so easily leads to dishonesty.**)

There was a part of me thinking that a forced position change would be another convenient excuse I could use for never seeing the field again. Yet another way to save face with my buddies back home. I could tell people things didn't work out when the new coach came along and told me I couldn't play *my* position anymore. Years could go by and I could be like one of those guys at the end of the bar talking about how much potential he had before some new coach came along and screwed him out of the position he was born to play. I could be like the guy who always talks about the blown-out knee that ended a career otherwise destined for nothing but glory and fame. Those stories sounded better than admitting I was too scared to play. Instead of being made fun of for being afraid, I could get sympathetic pats on the back for the rest of my life.

Self-pity can be alluring. I've now experienced enough life to know that some people feed off of the attention they get from one sob story after another.

"I want you at quarterback," Bud said. "I think you have the potential to eventually lead this offense. But you're holding yourself back. The QB is the leader of the offense. He's got to be confident and assertive. He's got to have a great attitude. He's got to make split-second decisions and he can't do that if he lacks confidence or if he's wallowing in the past and feeling bad about himself."

An awkward silence followed. I wasn't sure what he wanted me to say. I was embarrassed about the only time I played last season and my performance in the spring game hadn't done anything to convince me or anyone else that I was no longer a turnover machine.

I *was* afraid of taking the field in a real game. I *was* afraid of how badly I might embarrass myself again.

Bud placed a knuckle over his lips as he looked me over, like he was trying to read my mind. He then lowered his hand, rocked forward in his chair, and clapped his hands together, his elbows now on his desk.

"Okay, here's what I need from you," he said. "I need you to replace the memories you're calling up."

"Replace my memories?"

He nodded. "That's your summer assignment from me. I need you to take that Rice game and throw it away mentally. I imagine you've replayed it in your head enough times by now. You've learned all the valuable lessons you're gonna learn from it; now you're just replaying the humiliation of it over and over. It's time to give those memories the boot. Take all the negative comments you heard—from coaches, players, fans, girlfriends, uncles, whoever—and mentally wipe them all out."

"You want me to pretend the whole thing never happened?"

"Not exactly. We can't deny our pasts and pretend they never happened, but denying your past and dwelling on your past are two very different things. Mistakes were made and you have to own them, but you don't have to dwell on them. You don't have to beat yourself up over them.

"Danny, we *all* have regrets. We all wish we hadn't said or done certain things. We all wish we could take those things back. That's life. But since you can't go back and change those things, every minute you spend wishing you could is a complete waste of time.

"You don't have to be a victim of the past. You don't have to let it ruin your present or determine your future."

"I'm all ears," I said, anxious for a way to move on from that embarrassing afternoon still dominating my thoughts.

"Though you can't change the past, you can change the way you think about the past," Bud said. "A mistake is nothing more than a lesson to learn from. That's it. Once you learn the lesson it teaches, you have to move on and forget about it.

"Most people fixate on their screwups. They make a mistake and then beat themselves up about it for weeks, months, years. Happy people don't do that. Successful people don't do that. They move forward, not backward.

"You can't let a mistake beat you twice. When you dwell on a defeat in your head, you experience it over and over again. Each time you mentally replay it, you experience those negative feelings again. It brings you down. It stifles your confidence. The past defeat beats you

all over again.

"Instead, you need to look at mistakes like like the lessons you learn in school or in a book. ~ back from the feelings and emotions of those mistakes and see it from the perspective of someone objectively watching film: here's what happened, here's what you need to do in the future. Period. Done. Time to move on. You'll drive yourself crazy if you don't learn how to move on."

"I'll give it a try," I said, not hiding my skepticism.

"You can do it," Bud said. "Anyone can if they make the decision to.

"Whenever you start replaying those negative events in your head, ask yourself, 'What's the lesson I'm supposed to learn from this?' When you have your answer, move on and promise to do things differently next time. That's all replaying a past mistake is good for: learning the lesson for next time. Focus only on the lesson to be learned from the mistake. Just the lesson. Don't reexperience the emotions from that day. That will drive you crazy and keep you feeling down. Just learn the lesson. No further attachment."

"I wish I could," I said. "But I can't stop replaying that game in my head. How can I not feel embarrassed about the way I played? I want to go back and slap myself silly for making such stupid errors. Every time I think about that day, I'm either angry at myself for playing the way I did or I'm so humiliated I want to crawl into a hole. It literally makes my stomach queasy."

Uh-oh. I've said too much. So much for saving face and trying to look confident to my new coach. I just spilled my guts like I was talking to a shrink.

Bud leaned back with raised eyebrows and a smile, surprised at my frankness.

"I like your honesty, Danny. Saves me the trouble of spending the next six months trying to figure you out."

13

"I have always believed that what you expect is usually what you get, what you focus on is what you draw to yourself."

– Pete Carroll, Winner of 2 National Titles and 1 Super Bowl

"We all have our share of negative and positive memories from the past," Bud said. "Confident people choose to think mostly about the positive memories while insecure people choose to think mostly about the negative ones.

"**The ability to move on quickly from a past mistake is one of the secrets to being successful in whatever you do. It's also a secret to happiness and peace of mind.**

"You want to be happy in life? Stop dwelling on your worst moments. Stop thinking about the bad game you had, the test you flunked, that bully next door when you were a kid, that time mommy or daddy said you were no good. Everyone has bad memories like that, but you can't wallow in the self-pity of those bad moments.

"One of the key differences between happy people and unhappy people is how they think about their past. Happy people reminisce about the good times and the achievements they're proud of. Unhappy people ruminate on the bad times and the mistakes they're most embarrassed about."

The memory of my fumble into the end zone against Rice flashed before me. I saw myself on film, pulling out from under center with the football wobbling in my hands, then clasping my hands together, trying to secure the ball but only seeing it squirt from my hands and bounce towards the endzone. I see how silly I looked, awkwardly tripping over myself and falling to my knees as I tried to recover the fumble. Our game wasn't even on TV, but I imagined announcers laughing at me during the radio broadcast. My cheeks got hot. My stomach turned. I was so humiliated. So embarrassed.

"What are you thinking about right this moment?" Bud asked.

I told him.

"Okay," he said, "what's the lesson you need to learn from that fumble?"

"I need to make sure I secure the football before I pull away from the center. I was too hurried in that moment."

"There you go. That's a lesson you probably learned when you were eight years old, but you're never too old to remind yourself of it. I don't have to tell you that every single Hall of Fame quarterback in the history of this sport has muffed center exchanges. It's a mistake. It's a mistake that needs to be corrected. It's a mistake that teaches you a lesson. But that's all it is. A lesson. A lesson to learn from."

"But I can't stop replaying it," I said. "I can't stop hearing Coach Wyatt tell me I don't belong at this level."

"Here's what you do when you can't shake a bad memory," Bud said. "It doesn't work to just tell yourself, 'Stop thinking about it.' The more you tell yourself to stop thinking about the color red, the more you're gonna think about the color red. Instead, you have to replace the negative memory with something positive. Any time that memory starts to creep back into your mind, you have to slam the door on it and change it to one of your greatest memories.

"What's one of your favorite memories of playing ball in high school?"

I smiled. This was easy. "In our state championship game, we were down by four with a minute-ten left to play. We were on our own forty-yard line. We ran the option, I kept it. I broke a tackle at the forty-three, cut outside, stiff-armed a d-back at the fifty, and then raced down the sidelines. Nobody came close to catching me. I don't think I've ever run that fast in my life. It was like my cleats never hit the ground. We won the game. It was awesome. I'll never forget it."

"There you go," he said. "*Feel* those emotions. Focus on those feelings of success, of speed, of victory. What a great day that was. What a great play that was. The joy you felt.

The love you felt from your teammates and the fans. The confidence you felt inside as you ran into the endzone. Allow yourself to enjoy those feelings."

I felt lighter as one of the greatest memories of my life replayed in my mind.

"Now," Bud said. "Every time you start to dwell on a mistake you made against Rice or at any other time, I want you to stop yourself and change the channel. Picture a TV that you're literally changing the channel on. Change it to a replay of that state championship moment and *feel* that moment again.

"**You can dwell on a positive moment in your past just as easily as you can dwell on a negative moment.** Like everything else, the choice is yours."

I couldn't help but smile again as I recalled that glorious moment.

"From this point forward," Bud said, "I want you to consciously replace that negative memory with the positive memory you just told me about. That can be your go-to positive memory. Change the channel to that whenever a negative memory pops up.

"**Whatever you think about most will dominate your mental and emotional state. That means that whatever you think about most will determine what you experience right now *and* in the future.** That's why you must make positive memories your *dominant* memories. That's what I want you dwelling on. That's what I want you *feeling*.

"You know how rare it is to experience an awesome moment like the one you just described?" Bud chuckled. "I bet you felt strong enough to conquer the world."

I nodded. "It was a *great* moment."

"You've got to hold tight to that one," Bud said. "Embrace it. Relive it and let it fuel your emotions. Use it to bring yourself up whenever you're feeling down. When you do that, you'll soon be experiencing more moments just like it."

I felt energy rising up within me as I replayed that moment. *That's the kind of player I want to be*, I thought to myself. *That's the kind of player I am.*

"What you focus on most tends to come about," Bud said. "Focus on those great moments that made you feel *good* if you want to experience more like them in the future. Focus on the embarrassing moments of your past if those are the ones you want to experience more of.

"Whenever you catch yourself dwelling on something negative, change the channel. I bet you have several other great moments you can call up. Start reflecting on those. Build a mental highlight reel of some of your greatest moments, those times when you felt proud of yourself, those moments when you felt unstoppable. Feel your confidence rise as you reminisce on those experiences.

"Danny, you'll find that this technique works way beyond football. We all have embarrassing moments in our past. We all have moments where somebody we care about said or did something awful to us. We all have moments where *we* said or did something we wish we could take back. But dwelling on those negative memories only brings us down. They make us feel bad about ourselves, which makes us more likely to experience similar negative moments in the future."

I thought about one of the many times my mom told me I was "worthless." I caught myself and turned the channel to the time my high school coach told me I was "the greatest player" he ever coached.

"Choose to dwell on the positive memories of the past instead of the negative ones," Bud said. "I don't care if the negative times outnumber the positive times, you have plenty of positive experiences you can choose to dwell on instead. It's a choice. When a negative memory creeps into your mind, you *can* make the choice to change the channel and replace it with a positive one. That's what I want you to do."

I had walked into Bud Sullivan's office unsure about my future as a football player. I walked out with a level of confidence I had not felt since arriving on this campus two summers ago. It was that dramatic of a shift. This was a coach who didn't want me to pay for my past mistakes, he wanted me to learn from them and, most importantly, to move on from them.

Bud didn't promise me a bump in the depth chart. He didn't tell me I'd never make another mistake. He simply taught me how to move on from the worst memory of my football career.

I was now armed with a powerful technique that would benefit me my entire life.

It's not always easy to implement this "change the channel" technique. It's one I still have to work on today, but it's worth the effort. You have to make it a habit. You have to catch yourself when dwelling on something negative and then deliberately change the channel to something positive.

These days, as the host of a sports talk radio show that airs across the nation for three hours almost every weekday, I've had plenty of flubs heard by millions of people. There are times when I replay those flubs and cringe. I wonder what I was thinking—*How could I say something so stupid?* Sometimes I'll find a reason. Maybe I was rushing to make a point I had not fully thought through. Maybe I should have done more research before addressing a particular topic. Maybe I simply should have known when to keep my mouth shut. Or, maybe there was no reason at all and it was just one of those moments when the thought in my head didn't come out as I intended.

Whatever the reason—and even if there isn't one—I address the mistake and learn whatever I can from it. If an apology or clarification is necessary, I do it. But once that's done, I don't allow myself dwell on it. As soon as I notice I'm replaying (and reexperiencing) the cringeworthy moment, I mentally change the channel. I choose to think about some of my better moments on the air or even some of my happiest moments in other areas of life.

This technique works. I immediately feel happier and more confident. And confidence makes me better at my job going forward.

We all make mistakes or have negative memories that haunt us. No matter how hard you try, you can't forget about them. But you can *replace* the negative with something positive as soon as it comes up.

This technique was a gamechanger for me in college. It allowed me to break away from all kinds of negative memories that haunted my past. I applied it not only to my performance on the field, but also to hurtful things people said to me, poor tests in school, past rejections, memories of being made of fun as a kid, and memories of when I said or did regrettable things out of my own insecurities — *anything* negative that I was ruminating on.

Changing the channel on those memories altered the trajectory of my college football career and it continues to be an invaluable tool in my life today.

14

"I think the most important thing of all for any team is a winning attitude. Coaches must have it. The players must have it."

– Bear Bryant, 6-Time National Champion Football Coach

Over the next several months, I forced myself to stop dwelling on my worst moments and to instead focus on the positive things I had done as a quarterback. The more I focused on the positives of my past, the more I saw myself as a worthy player in the present.

As I changed the way I thought of myself, a new goal emerged for what I wanted to accomplish. No longer did I want to hide at the end of the bench. I now wanted to become the very best quarterback I was capable of becoming. I wanted to work my way up the depth chart and prove I was capable of playing, perhaps even starting, at this level. I wanted to redeem myself.

I wish I could say that with renewed confidence and an ironclad belief in myself, I powered through summer conditioning and two-a-day practices to earn the starting

the 1987 season began. I wish I could say the
.....n united as one and caught the entire nation by
surprise with a jaw-dropping single-season turnaround
that everyone still talks about today. I wish I could say we
all bought into Bud Sullivan's message of confidence, team
unity, and enthusiasm, and that none of us struggled with
insecurity, selfishness, or pessimism ever again.

On second thought, maybe I don't wish I could say that.
Because that's not how progress is made. Impactful change
rarely happens overnight. It's a journey. A challenging
journey that never really ends.

When the season began, I had mentally shifted from
being afraid to take the field to actually *wanting* to work my
up the depth chart. However, I remained third on the depth
chart, behind Jerry Miller and Mike Pederson, after
preseason practices. They were both getting better at
running the wishbone offense and I think Bud liked being
able to air it out a little more than he was used to. On top of
that, a freshman quarterback named Reggie Coleman
arrived in August. He needed to put on some weight and
learn Bud's offense, but it was clear I was no longer the
fastest QB on the roster. Reggie was an amazing athlete.

As for our team, we stumbled out of the gate. Our first
game was on the road against Florida State, a team ranked
No. 8 in the preseason. We were enthusiastic heading into
the game and Jerry managed to lead us on a few long, clock-
chewing drives that kept things close in the first half. But in

the second half, the Seminoles pulled away. They had too much firepower and we lost, 45-14. Florida State would end up finishing the season 11-1 and ranked No. 2 in the nation.

In week two, we traveled to Oklahoma State and lost, 35-17. The Cowboys were unranked at the time, but would end up winning ten games and finishing the year ranked No. 11.

We finally had a home game in week three as we welcomed Southwest Texas State, a Division 1-AA team (that was a division below us with fewer scholarships, lower budgets, and smaller schools). The Bobcats were coming off a 4-7 season and it was the one game on the schedule everyone predicted we'd win. It was a miserably hot and humid day and only something like 9,000 fans showed up (a crowd size that was on par at the time with local *high school* games). Jerry left the game in the third quarter with an ankle injury and our offense struggled to move the ball with Mike at QB. We scored all of our points in the first half and hung on for a 20-17 win after the Bobcats missed a field goal attempt in the final seconds.

The Bud Sullivan era was not off to an impressive start. Our one victory wasn't a surprise (even the Wade Wyatt teams managed to beat the Division 1-AA teams on the schedule), but it was an uglier performance than expected. The new offense sputtered along with starts and stops, never really finding its rhythm. Led by Brian at middle linebacker, the defense started each of those first three games strong, but once the opposing team scored a touchdown or two, it felt like the levee broke and a surge of points followed.

Through the rocky start, Bud and his staff kept an upbeat attitude. I saw Bud get plenty frustrated at times, even throwing his headset once, but never did he resort to demeaning us. He never put us down. He'd call us out when we hung our heads and he'd let us know loud and clear if our effort was falling short of his expectations, but he never kicked us while we were down. In fact, it was just the opposite. He lifted us up. He kept telling us he believed in us and knew we were capable of so much more.

But how long could he keep up this enthusiasm?

We entered Southwest Conference play with a four-year conference losing streak intact. Our first SWC game was a 27-7 loss at home against No. 15 Texas A&M. It was actually a closer game than the scoreboard indicated. We missed what would have been a game-tying field goal early in the fourth quarter before the Aggies scored seventeen points in the final ten minutes.

It was our trip to Austin in week five where Bud was on the verge of losing the team. From my vantage point on the sidelines against Texas, I saw a lot of head-hanging, a lot of arguing between teammates, a lot of mistakes (*six* turnovers), and a general sense of guys checking out. I wasn't the only one who noticed this. It was obvious to anyone watching. The Longhorns gave us a 41-6 beatdown.

Just like that, we were 1-4 with two SWC losses as we headed into a bye week. *The Joline Post* expressed the sentiment perfectly with its Sunday-morning headline after the Texas game: *MORE OF THE SAME.*

How we responded would be a pivotal moment for our team and for the Bud Sullivan era.

15

"At some point, you just have to decide you're going to be confident. Then, as you do, you're going to have more success."

– Mike Leach, 2-Time College Football National Coach of the Year

What comes first, confidence or success?

There's no doubt that success breeds confidence. It's easier to feel good about yourself when things are going your way. But what if you haven't been winning? How do you start the turnaround? How do you generate the confidence that leads to wins? These were the questions Bud was about to answer for us.

The first practice after the Texas game, you could sense the team was deflated and frustrated. There were more mistakes than normal, as if they had carried over from Saturday's game. There were a few pushing-and-shoving incidents between teammates. A lot of guys were just going through the motions.

Bud had come to Arkansas A&M with a level of enthusiasm and positivity that many of us had never seen before. It was exciting. A fresh start. A promise that things would be different. Now, that enthusiasm was fading. It didn't matter who the new coach was or what his attitude was, we were still losers—one of the worst teams in all of Division 1-A college football.

With about thirty minutes left in practice, Bud had seen enough. He blew his whistle and stopped everything. He gathered the entire team at the center of the practice field and told us to take a knee.

"I've got something I want to say," Bud said, a stern look on his face. "Everyone on this team needs to *stop* feeling sorry for themselves."

This got our attention. We expected another rah-rah motivational speech from our upbeat coach, but Bud's tone was firm as he called us out.

"On Saturday afternoon, I saw guys with their heads hanging," he said. "I saw guys acting like they didn't want to be here. I saw guys giving half the effort they're capable of giving. Things got really bad in the second half. I saw guys giving up. Quitting.

"Each one of you knows, in your heart, if what I'm saying describes you. You know if you fought to the end on Saturday or if you checked out and quit. And just so we're clear, giving anything less than your best effort is the same as quitting. It's quitting on yourself and it's quitting on your brothers who depend on you."

He paused and looked us over. Brian had taken a knee

just to my left and didn't say a thing. Normally, this would be the moment where he'd whisper something sarcastic or at least huff and roll his eyes. Instead, he had a face of stone, his eyes focused downward. He had zero tackles against Texas, his worst game as a starter.

"Today, I'm seeing more of the same," Bud continued. "I'm watching guys quit.

"You want to know why people quit on something they love? There's only one reason. It's because they feel sorry for themselves.

"People don't quit because something is too hard. I've told you all a hundred times, doing something hard is fun and exciting. If it's something you love, like this game we're all so passionate about, you *embrace* the hard work. There's nothing like that feeling of achievement when you accomplish something hard. Of all the kids who love playing football growing up, do you know how few of them get to be in your shoes playing Division 1 college football? You all have spent your whole lives working to get to where you are. Hard work is in your DNA. You wouldn't have made it this far if you couldn't handle hard work. That's how I know you didn't quit because things got too hard on Saturday.

"And you didn't quit because you're weren't good enough. Every single Saturday when two teams take the field, one team will end up losing. That's football. That's life. But that doesn't mean the losing team quits. You can give your best and fail to accomplish your objective. Failing and quitting are two entirely different things. I can handle failure because that's something we can learn and grow from. I can't handle quitting.

"**The only reason anyone quits something they would otherwise love to do is because they start feeling sorry for themselves.** They start thinking, 'Poor me, what's the use? I guess I don't have what it takes. I guess it isn't meant to be.'

"**Self-pity is the enemy of self-confidence. It is the most powerful opposing force that prevents you from turning things around.**

"Self-pity not only makes you justify quitting; it makes you crave the sympathy you'll get for doing so. You start telling yourself that nobody has to deal with what you have to deal with. You imagine all the sympathy you're going to get from your mom or your dad or your girlfriend or whoever.

"Self-pity is toxic. The longer you wallow in it, the worse it gets." Bud's voice was getting louder. His face was reddening.

"I saw self-pity on Saturday. I saw guys feeling sorry for themselves. I saw guys who couldn't wait to get back home and have someone pat them on the back and say, 'Wow, you're right, you didn't have a chance out there. The deck was stacked against you. I'm impressed you made it as long as you did.'

"I saw self-pity on Saturday and I'm seeing it today."

Bud shook his head back and forth and then grabbed the hat he was wearing. "No more!" He slammed his hat to the ground in fury. I had never seen him this angry before.

"No more excuses," he said. "No more feeling sorry for yourselves because of what happened in the past. No more self-pity. And no more quitting!

"It breaks my heart to see you quit. It breaks my heart because it's a choice you're making. Everyone makes the choice to fight or quit and most of you chose to quit on Saturday.

"No more. Never again. I simply will not tolerate quitting."

The only sound was the wind blowing. I heard no sighs or whispers, nobody chiming in to disagree with Bud. I didn't even hear the sound of pads adjusting. Everyone was still. Bud had called out the team and we knew he was right.

We had quit on Saturday. Realizing *why* we quit, that it was self-pity — choosing to feel sorry for ourselves — was an eye-opening message.

"Fellas, we are five games into this season and we've got six more to go. If some of you have lost your passion for the game, then maybe it's time to go do something else with your life. But if you love this game and you want to be part of something special, the worst thing you can do is quit on yourself and this team. All of you have the talent to be so much better than what you're showing out on the field.

"I don't care what the scoreboard says (
record is. We could be winning by twenty (
twenty. We could be five-and-oh or oh-and-five
because that's all in the past. All I care about right now is
seeing everybody on this team give everything they've got.
You can't let the last game or the last play beat you twice.
You've got to move forward. You've got to believe in
yourself, sacrifice for each other, and attack each day with
confidence and enthusiasm. It's *your* choice."

Bud lowered his eyes.

"I can't walk over to each of you and hand you the
confidence you need. You have to choose it for yourself.
**You have to choose to believe that things are going to go
your way beginning with the very next play. You have to
choose to believe that good things are going to happen
because you're going to go out and *make* them happen.**

"Confident people don't feel sorry for themselves.
Confident people don't quit.

"**At some point, regardless of what has happened in
the past or what you're dealing with right this moment,
you have to *choose* to be confident. You have to choose to
believe in yourself. As soon as you do, everything
changes. It's like a magical switch gets flipped.**

"It's time to flip that switch. Choose to believe that good
things are going to happen.

"You've earned the right to be confident with the hard
work you put in this offseason and the preparation that

goes into each practice. Don't overanalyze it or second-guess whether you deserve to be confident. **Just do it. Believe. Choose to believe that things are going to start going your way and they will!**

"A person's performance will eventually match his or her confidence level. When you believe in yourself, good things start happening. I don't know exactly how or why it happens that way, but it does.

"I see too many of you looking around and waiting for something good to happen. You're waiting for somebody to make a big play or some good fortune to fall in your lap. You're looking at the scoreboard or worrying about our record. You're thinking, when things start turning around *then* you'll be more confident.

"But it doesn't work like that. **You have to choose to be confident first.** You have to tell yourself, 'Things are turning my way. I'm gonna make a big play. I'm gonna have the game of my life. I can handle anything that comes my way. I will give my very best and nobody can stop me!'

"When you talk to yourself like that, you're choosing to be confident. And when you choose to be confident, good things start happening.

"Self-pity will not be tolerated on this team. No more feeling sorry for yourselves, as if you have no control over what happens to you. And no more waiting around for confidence to find you. You must flip the switch and decide *right now* to be confident.

"Maybe that sounds risky to you. Maybe you think if you do that, you'll end up disappointed. Maybe you think you don't deserve to be confident.

"Forget all that. **Drop the self-doubt and the self-pity. Stop worrying about anything that happened in the past. Just go out and decide to be confident** *now*. **Decide to believe in yourself** *now*!

"I promise, you will not be disappointed."

Bud leaned over, picked up his hat, and swatted it against his leg a few times. Dust flickered off it. He put it back on his head and said, "Your assignment right now is simple. Flip the switch. Don't overanalyze it, don't question it, just do it. *Choose* to be confident. Believe that things will get better. Decide that *you* will make things better. Make the decision and see what happens. That's all I'm asking.

"From now on, every time you put on that Bulldog helmet, I want you to visualize flipping a switch. I want you to use it as a reminder to *choose* confidence."

Bud let out a frustrated sigh. "If you won't choose to be confident, you might as well not suit up with us again."

He walked off the practice field, still looking angry. The assistant coaches followed. Practice was over. The message was clear.

Up to that point, despite all the times Bud had talked about confidence being a choice, I still thought it was something that would eventually come to me. I thought it was something that would grow as good things happened.

But here was Bud telling us we had to choose confidence right now, regardless of whatever results we were experiencing at the moment. He was telling us to do something most people would call reckless. He was telling us to believe in ourselves *before* we had the results to back up that belief.

He promised us, if we *decided* to believe in ourselves, positive results would follow.

He was right.

16

"The measure of who we are is how we react to something that doesn't go our way."

– Gregg Popovich, 5-Time NBA Champion Coach

Learning to *choose* confidence and not wait around for it was a turning point for me and most of the team.

The night after Bud's talk about self-pity and flipping the switch, I expected Brian to blow it off like he always did, maybe make another joke about "Coach Pollyanna." Instead, he barely said a word back in our dorm room. We were both studying when he broke the silence.

"I will say this, Bud makes you think."

When we addressed our head coach, we called him, *Coach*, but when talking with each other, he was always, *Bud*.

I nodded. "He made some good points today."

"That he did," Brian said. "You know, this game has always come pretty easy to me. I think I was born to play football. But there are times when I get so frustrated out on the field. Times when I feel like I'm having to do everything and nobody else is picking up the slack. I know that sounds arrogant, and I suppose it is, but it's the truth. I felt that way in high school and I've felt that way this year.

"On Saturday, Texas was keying on me. They were double-teaming me all day. And I swear, the refs were letting them get away with holding. After that first quarter, I could see how the game was going to go. It didn't matter what I did, I was going to get taken out of the play and nobody else was going to step up."

I winced at the comment. It sounded so arrogant. But I also knew it was true.

"I know I sound like a whiner saying this," Brian said. "I used to say the same stuff to my coach in high school, complaining that nobody else was pulling their weight. But not until today did I realize that an attitude like that is not only arrogant, it's pathetic. It's self-pity. I can try to act like I'm so good that I have some right to whine about everybody else, but the truth is, I'm feeling sorry for myself, aren't I?"

My silence served as my response.

Brian nodded. "You know it and I know it. Bud is right. I was out there wallowing in self-pity. Instead of stepping up to the challenge and playing my ass off when the going got tough, I felt sorry for myself and started blaming my teammates, the refs, everyone else.

"I wonder how I would've played if I had just decided,

at that moment, to be a difference maker. What if during the Texas game I had said, 'Okay, this is how it's gonna be? Well, bring it on. Give me your best. You can double-team me, you can triple-team me, you can hold me, you can block me in the back, it doesn't matter. I *am* gonna make a play!'

"What if I had said that to myself? What if instead of backing down in self-pity I had chosen to be confident?"

"Could've been a different game," I said.

"Maybe it would've turned out different or maybe it wouldn't have. But either way, I would have known that I left it all on the field. I would've known I had given it everything I had. I would've given my best and seen where I stood. But I didn't. I quit. I quit on myself and I quit on the team."

Brian, a guy who was almost always clowning around and making jokes in any situation, was as serious as I had ever seen him. He was staring at the wall in front of him, undoubtedly replaying Saturday's poor performance in his mind. His fist was gripped around the pencil he was holding and his knuckles were white. At that moment, he looked intense enough to put on the pads and run through an opposing offense.

He turned my way. "Danny, Bud was right and I am never going to do that again. I love this game. Who knows how many Saturdays any of us have left? I'm never gonna play that way again. I will never quit again."

Though he wouldn't officially be voted a team captain

until the next season, that was the moment in my mind where Brian Dawson shifted from team clown to team leader. He would continue to have a good time and joke around (that was his personality), but on the field Brian was never again pushed around. I never again saw him take a play off — in practice or in a game.

Bud now had the most talented player on the team in his corner. Others would follow.

Our team changed that night.

17

"Confident leaders freely admit their own mistakes. And by doing it publicly, set an example for others to take responsibility."

– Bill Parcells, 2-Time Super Bowl Champion Coach

I am confident.

I believe in myself.

Good things are coming my way.

I choose to make things happen.

Repeating these statements over and over again had a tremendous impact on the way I carried myself on and off the field. Reminding myself that confidence was a choice and it was up to me to decide whether I would or would not be confident was an empowering realization.

The more I repeated these phrases, the more confident I felt inside.

During practices, I felt faster on my feet and I made quicker decisions. I still had mishaps, but I shook them off and *decided* to be confident anyway, telling myself I would improve on the next play. And more often than not, I did improve.

In the weight room, I felt stronger and continued to make progress.

Off the field, I was walking a bit taller and noticed myself smiling at strangers. I used to have the tendency to lower my eyes and keep to myself when approaching people I didn't know. I suppose I was afraid if I was outgoing and friendly and they didn't return my friendliness, I'd feel rejected; it would hurt my pride. Now, I didn't care. I was choosing to be confident regardless. (It turned out, most people returned my friendliness.)

I also started talking with Sherry again. I saw her on campus one day and a message from one of our Sunday night meetings had popped into my head.

Bud had told us, "**Admitting when you are wrong is a sign of confidence. People with brittle egos can never admit when they're wrong. Confident people are secure enough in themselves to be honest about their mistakes and regrets. They don't hide, they don't blame others, and they don't try to cover it up. They own their mistakes and they're willing to ask for forgiveness when necessary.**"

When I saw Sherry, I told her I was sorry for the way I had acted over the last two years. "I'm not trying to win you back," I said, though I did miss her and hoped that someday we could give it another shot. "I just want you to know I realize what a jerk I was being and I'm trying to be a better man."

As I walked away, she said, "Thanks, Danny. That means a lot."

I turned back, smiled, and waved.

As I continued walking, she shouted, "Give me a call sometime."

I did exactly that a couple days later. We weren't dating, but we were talking again. That alone felt good. Sherry had been my best friend for three years stretching back to high school.

On the football field, not everyone was choosing confidence. Three more players left the team after meetings with Bud. A handful of others remained technically on the team, but they weren't buying into Bud's message and had mentally checked out. Those guys, two of them starters, lost more and more playing time and eventually never saw the field again. Bud was not going to let negative people undermine his message and bring the rest of the team down.

As I played with renewed confidence, I got the sense Mike Pederson was one of the guys who had checked out. Though he had been the number two QB on the depth chart since the start of the season and had made progress picking up Bud's option offense, I could tell he was never comfortable running with the ball. The two times Mike had seen action in a game after Jerry left with an injury, the offense stalled out. Mike even confided in me a few times how unhappy he was with this offense, saying he wished he could pass the ball more.

At practice, Mike was regressing and I started getting more reps.

Sure enough, when the depth chart prior to the Houston game was posted, I was bumped up to the number two QB spot.

18

"First you win the battle in your mind. Next you win the battle in practice. Then (and only then) you win the battle in the game."

– Urban Meyer, 3-Time National Champion Football Coach

The Houston game was a magical moment for Arkansas A&M football.

The Cougars had also hired a new head coach prior to the season. His name was Jack Pardee and he brought in an innovative, wide-open offense called the run-and-shoot. The transition to this new offense was taking some time and Houston had stumbled out of the gate. Both our teams entered the game with a record of 1-4.

Though it was Homecoming for us, we once again played in front of an embarrassingly small crowd. But that didn't matter. Bud's talk during the bye week after the Texas game ignited some of our best practices ever. We were a new team, though nobody outside our locker room knew it. The old Arkansas A&M team was dead and buried. We couldn't wait to prove it.

We took a 14-10 lead into halftime. In the third quarter, Houston's offense started clicking. They drove down the field fast to take a 17-14 lead. After a fumbled snap on third down led to a punt, Houston again scored a quick touchdown and led, 24-14, just like that.

This was usually the time when our offensive players would hang their heads and our defense would start surrendering points. But things were different on this day.

On our next series, I watched from the sidelines as Jerry executed a perfectly-read option pitch to our halfback and after a key downfield block by one of our receivers, there was nothing but green grass in front of him as he sprinted seventy-one yards for a touchdown. We had closed Houston's lead to three points.

The defense took the field and on a crucial third-and-four play, Houston threw a swing pass to their running back and Brian delivered a big hit two yards short of the first down. We scored on the next drive to retake the lead, 28-24.

Both teams traded field goals after that. Late in the fourth quarter we were leading, 31-27, but Houston's offense found its rhythm. Quick passes drove the Cougars to our thirteen-yard line with just three minutes left to play.

On first down, their quarterback dropped back and fired a pass over the middle. Brian read the play perfectly. He dropped deeper than normal into coverage, but then shot in front of the receiver's slant route and picked the ball off at the seven. He was moving so fast that he was running past the original line of scrimmage before most of Houston's players realized he had the ball. Brian showcased his speed as he returned the interception ninety-three yards for a touchdown.

The fans in attendance went nuts. Our sidelines did as well.

The defense sealed our 38-27 victory with a fourth-down stop on the next series. When the clock hit all zeros, we poured Gatorade on Bud and the student section stormed the field. Our four-year Southwest Conference losing streak was over. You would have thought we won the Super Bowl the way we celebrated that day.

The winning momentum carried us into the next week when we upset Baylor, 14-7. We beat TCU the week after that, 20-16.

Just like that, we were 4-4 and had a three-game *winning* streak in the Southwest Conference.

19

"When you have confidence, you can have a lot of fun. When you have fun, you can do amazing things."

– Joe Namath, Hall of Fame Quarterback and Super Bowl III MVP

The first Saturday in November, our three-game SWC winning streak came to an end when we lost to Texas Tech. We played hard, but lost by a touchdown.

Despite the loss, our team remained confident. We were playing better and knew it. Reviewing the film, we saw we were just a few plays away from a different outcome. The coaches were constructive. They reminded us how the loss would help us grow as a team *if* we chose to learn from it instead of beating ourselves up.

"How you choose to respond to adversity determines where you end up," Bud told us. "It's all about your response. **You can't always control the events in life, but you *can* always control how you respond to those events.**"

At 4-5 and with two games to go, we still had a shot at finishing the season with a winning record — a notion that would have seemed ludicrous just six months earlier. And with a winning record would come the possibility of a bowl game invitation. Arkansas A&M had only been to two bowl games in school history, the last one in 1961.

The practice week leading up to our tenth game of the season went along as normal until a Wednesday afternoon scrimmage changed everything.

We were working on a goal-line situation near the end of practice. Jerry Miller, our staring quarterback, kept the ball on an option play. He noticed a crease between two defenders and tried to shoot through the gap. The gap closed quickly and Jerry hit the ground just short of the goal line. Nothing seemed out of the ordinary until Jerry got up and started walking back to the huddle. He took three tentative steps before falling to the ground and grabbing his left knee.

Jerry left with the trainers and I handled the remaining snaps at practice. Later that night, Bud told me Jerry was done for the year and I would be the starter on Saturday.

After an initial jolt of excitement, I felt my stomach sink as fear rushed in.

It's one thing to be Mr. Confident when you're the backup and there isn't any pressure on you; it's quite another when you're the starting quarterback and the entire offense depends on you not screwing things up, which is exactly what I had done the last time I started for this team.

Our tenth game would be on the road against Rice. The

significance of facing Rice in my first game back as the starter wasn't lost on me. The "Rice Game" had been seared into my mind as the single worst moment of my athletic career and the most embarrassing afternoon of my life. While I was getting better at "changing the channel" on memories of that day, I couldn't block it out completely and the game still haunted me from time to time.

There were two ways I could approach facing the exact same team that had stolen my dignity a year ago. I could see it as a tremendous opportunity to redeem myself. Or, I could allow the fear of humiliating myself again take over my mind.

Obviously, I *wanted* to redeem myself, but in the nights leading up to the game I couldn't stop replaying those humiliating moments from a year ago. I again tried to "change the channel" and replace those memories as soon as they came up, but it was harder to do as game time approached.

I also realized this could be my last chance to play quarterback at this level. If I played at all like I did last time, I'd surely be benched and never given another opportunity.

I was feeding my fears and increasing the pressure on myself.

On paper, we were expected to beat Rice. The Owls were 2-7 and had not won a SWC game. We were 4-5 and had won three of our last four conference games. But the memories of how badly I had played the last time we faced

Rice overshadowed everything else in my mind. In the hotel room the night before the game, I could barely sleep.

It was a drizzly afternoon with sporadic showers in Houston, where we'd be playing Rice on a slippery green carpet (thank God stadiums have since moved on from the old style of artificial turf that once blanketed so many football fields back in the '70s, '80s, and '90s — the stuff felt like green-painted cement and could turn slick as an ice rink in even the slightest rainy conditions). The wet weather was ideal for mishandling a slippery football and visions of me loosing hold of the ball flashed through my mind.

Going through warmups prior to the game, Bud could see something was wrong with me.

He pulled me aside and said, "Remember that state championship game you told me about?"

I nodded.

"*That's* the kind of performance you're gonna have today," he said. "You are not the quarterback you were the last time you played against this team. You were made to run this offense and you are gonna have a big game today as long as you *decide* to have one.

"Don't second-guess yourself. Don't get caught up in fears or negative memories. Play *today's* game. This is your moment. Decide right now the type of quarterback you're gonna be. However you see yourself, that's how you will play today.

"I believe in you, Danny. You're my quarterback no

matter what happens out there today. Don't worry about a thing, just go out there and have fun!"

"You got it, Coach," I said, now seeing myself in a more positive light.

Bud had flipped the switch for me. He was throwing his full support behind me and alleviating my fears.

For a moment, I saw myself back in high school, racing down the sidelines on my way to a touchdown. I then remembered breaking a big run in practice the other day. Finally, I envisioned myself throwing a perfect pass *today*, on *this* field.

When we broke the huddle for the first time that afternoon, I had butterflies in my stomach, but it wasn't because I was imagining mistakes. It was the normal nervousness you feel when you're about to do something important—half adrenaline and half fear, fight or flight battling it out within. I took a deep breath, which calmed my nerves.

The first play was a simple double-iso call where all I had to do was hand the ball to one of our halfbacks while the fullback and other halfback led the way with lead blocks. I took the snap clean and pulled away from the center with no problem, but I must have been too hyped up, moving too fast. As I turned to hand the ball to the appropriate halfback, it slipped out of my hands and banged into his knee. The ball bounced towards the line of scrimmage.

This can't be happening again.

I dove on the loose ball and recovered the fumble, limiting the damage. Still, I could not believe I had *again* fumbled the ball on my first play from scrimmage.

On second-and-twelve, we called a triple-option play. Whether I misread the defense or just panicked, I gave the ball to my first option read, the fullback diving forward, and he was stuffed a yard behind the line of scrimmage.

It was now third down and a long thirteen yards to go for the first. Our receiver ran in from the sidelines to give me the play call. It was a pass. He told me the play and said, "Coach said to stop thinking and just play. Believe in yourself and have fun." He then gave me a pat on the shoulder pads and hustled to his place in the huddle.

Bud is right, I thought as I took a deep breath. *I must choose to believe in myself.*

I called the play and we broke the huddle. As I got behind center, I told myself, *Have fun. Be confident.*

The ball was snapped and I dropped back to pass. My first target was covered. My second target had a step on his man, but the space between the two was closing fast.

I noticed a Rice defensive end closing in from my left as I surveyed the field. I took two steps forward with my arm cocked and ready to throw the ball. Then I saw the battling linemen in front of me widen out and a large gap of green turf opened up between them.

Not thinking, just playing, I tucked the ball and took off

straight ahead. Once in the open field, I made a linebacker miss. A defensive back sprinted towards me as I broke to the right side of the field. He dove at my legs, but instead of tripping me up I was able to keep my balance and his momentum actually pushed me forward as he hit the wet turf. I let me legs do the rest. Like that great moment back in high school, I don't remember my shoes hitting the ground as I glided up the sidelines for an eighty-three-yard touchdown run.

As I crossed the goal line, I felt lighter than ever, a massive weight lifting off my shoulders. My teammates greeted me in the end zone and we hugged in celebration.

It was pure joy — a joy I had not felt in three years. It was as though all the demons that had been haunting me were suddenly banished far away.

From that point forward, I was a new man. I had told myself to be confident. I had told myself to believe I could compete at this level. Now, I had finally proved it to myself.

The rest of the afternoon was some of the most fun I ever had on a football field. It was one of those games where it felt like we could do no wrong, on both offense and defense. I ended up rushing for 147 yards and three touchdowns. Passing the ball, I completed eight of my twelve attempts for seventy-six yards (not exactly Heisman-winning numbers, but we *were* an option team) and, most importantly, I didn't throw any interceptions.

I wasn't perfect. I made some poor reads on a few of our

option plays and I fumbled the ball again in the third quarter (though I recovered it quickly), but I was having fun. I was playing with confidence and joy. We all were.

We won the game, 35-7, and I don't think I stopped smiling the whole trip home. We were 5-5, one win away from a winning season and a potential bowl trip.

20

"Confidence is completely ours to give to ourselves, and ours to take away when we feel low. If we've lost it, we simply must find it again."

– Joe Montana, 4-Time Super Bowl Champion Quarterback

Football, like life, often feels like a roller coaster. The ups shift to downs and back again faster than you're prepared for. You're riding high one practice, one game, or one play, and you're plunging to a new low the next.

Everything can change in an instant.

Years after my playing days were over, Bud would tell me, **"Confidence doesn't prevent life from throwing adversity at you. Nothing will prevent that. But confidence *will* help you overcome whatever adversity comes your way."**

Our final game of the 1987 regular season was on the road against Arkansas. The Razorbacks entered the game with a record of 7-3 and they were holding onto second place in the Southwest Conference standings.

Despite our improvement, nobody outside our locker room expected us to beat our in-state foe.

Historically, this was a lopsided series. Arkansas A&M had not defeated Arkansas since 1967 and our losing streak wasn't expected to end on this day.

Like us, Arkansas ran an option offense. The similarity of our offenses meant the Razorback defense was much more familiar with our scheme than most other opponents. All day long, our offense struggled to find daylight. Every time I spotted a gap in the defense, it would close fast. Their defensive linemen and linebackers did a great job of disguising their responsibilities, which made it hard for me to make proper option reads. At other times, their bigger and faster defenders simply overwhelmed our blockers.

We tried to grind out drives three and four yards at a time, but too often we'd get stuffed at the line of scrimmage and lose yardage. We ended up facing a lot of third-and-long situations, which is a big problem for an option offense.

After three quarters, our offense had managed just two field goals. I had run the ball for an unimpressive twenty-one yards on fourteen carries and completed only three of my ten pass attempts. As each drive ended, I grew more frustrated with my inability to break a big play. I was feeling out of my league.

Thanks to our defense, we were still in the game, trailing 17-6. But time was running out.

With just over ten minutes left to play, we finally got the break we needed on offense. On a fairly routine off-tackle run, our halfback broke a tackle and rumbled for a thirty-six-yard gain, our biggest offensive play of the day. We then powered our way down to the Arkansas five-yard line thanks to two fourth-down conversions.

On third-and-goal from the five, we ran a bootleg play where I faked a handoff and rolled out to the right side of the field looking for a receiver. My tight end broke free on a shallow corner route and I hit him in the endzone for a touchdown. It was my first touchdown pass at the college level and it closed Arkansas' lead to five points. We went for the two-point conversion to pull within three, but their defense stopped our running back short of the goal line on a counter.

We trailed the Razorbacks, 17-12, with a little more than five minutes left in the game. If our defense could make a stop, we had a chance to do the unthinkable.

After giving up two first downs, the defense forced a punt and our offense took over with 2:21 left to play. We started the drive from our own thirty-two-yard line and I had visions of marching our team down the field for a last-second victory.

We had to hurry. This wasn't the time to grind it out with our option attack. We would have to pass our way down the field if we wanted to score in time.

I tried to be calm and confident, but everyone in the

stadium knew I was not a skilled passer. I threw three-straight incomplete passes before somehow managing to complete an eighteen-yard pass on fourth-and-ten.

The next drive was almost identical. Three more incomplete passes and another fourth-down conversion — this one a pass that got tipped by an Arkansas defender before our receiver caught the ball and galloped to a twenty-six-yard gain.

We now had the ball at the Razorback twenty-four-yard line with 0:56 left to play.

On first down, I dropped back to pass. A defensive end got loose and charged into our backfield. I side-stepped him and moved forward. I was still looking to throw the ball when another defender blindsided me and drove me into the turf as the Arkansas crowd roared. It was a three-yard loss and we had to burn our last timeout to stop the clock.

On the sidelines, Bud went over what the next two plays would be and how we should react to different scenarios. He then looked at me, smiled big as he slapped me on the shoulder and said, "You got this, Danny."

On second-and-thirteen from the twenty-seven-yard line, I again dropped back to pass. First target was covered. I checked down to the next and saw he had been pushed wide on his route. I scrambled to my right to buy some time as my receiver recovered and worked his way past the defender. He was picking up speed and now had his man beat. The defense was closing in on me. I had my eyes locked on my number two receiver as he raced to the end zone with what was now two steps on his man.

This was it. This was the type a moment every quarterback dreams about.

I cocked my arm back and let the ball fly. It was a perfect arch, like something a *passing* quarterback would throw.

My receiver looked back, saw the ball coming. He stretched out his arms. The ball was going to hit him in stride…

Then, out of nowhere, a Razorback defender jumped high in front of the ball and snagged it out of the air.

The defender caught the ball and stepped out of bounds in the end zone. The Razorback home crowd erupted with cheers.

Interception.

Touchback.

Arkansas ball.

Game over.

It was the free safety who had raced over to make the interception. I was so locked in on my receiver beating the cornerback who was covering him that I never noticed the free safety who had been playing the middle of the field up top. I was baited into throwing that pass.

I had blown our chance at finally beating Arkansas, finally having a winning season, and finally going to a bowl game. We lost the game because of my awful decision.

In the locker room after the game, Bud told us, "You win

some and you lose some, you all know that. But you went down swinging. Nobody quit. Not a single player on this team quit. That's all I care about. This team has set the tone for a future of greatness at Arkansas A&M. You all have nothing to hang your heads about."

But I couldn't help but hang my head on the bus ride back to Joline. *How did I overlook that free safety? Why didn't I throw the ball to my receiver's outside shoulder instead of letting it float inside? Why didn't I throw the ball away and move onto another down? Why did I force it? This team lost the biggest game of the season because of me.*

My teammates tried to be supportive and say the right things. They gave me the typical lines about keeping my head up and not blaming myself. But I could see in their eyes I had let them down. They had counted on me in the biggest moment of the season and I had let them down.

21

"To live in the past is to die in the present."

– Bill Belichick, 6-Time Super Bowl Champion Coach

After the loss to Arkansas, I felt terrible about myself. We had come so close to winning and I blamed myself for the loss. The season was over and there was no *next game* to look forward to. All those voices saying things like, "You don't belong in college, you can't compete at this level, who do you think you are?" came roaring back into my mind.

I didn't go to class the Monday after the Arkansas game, I was too embarrassed. Sherry called me on Tuesday to see how I was doing, but I didn't return the call for the same reason. I was trying to avoid the world.

On Wednesday, I tried to snap myself out of my funk by *changing the channel* and replacing the memory of my interception with one of my more positive plays, just like Bud had taught me to do. But the game-losing interception against Arkansas was too fresh, too powerful. I couldn't suppress it. "What's the use?" I muttered to myself. "It's not going to change what happened."

Thursday morning, we were supposed to be back in the weight room after a few days off. I thought about not showing up, maybe claiming to be sick, but I knew that would be trouble. I forced myself to face the world again.

"Coach Sullivan wants to see you," Coach Stonebreaker said as soon as I stepped foot in the football facility. "He's waiting in the film room."

Uh-oh.

I had skipped several classes that week. Not only was that a violation of team rules, but it was also something a guy like me couldn't afford to do. I needed to get my grades up and skipping class wasn't going to help.

When I got to the film room, Bud was watching tape of another Arkansas game, already scouting for next season. I took a seat across the table. Bud paused the tape and turned to me.

"We all make mistakes," he said. "We all suffer disappointments. It's how one responds to those setbacks that separates the winners from the losers. The worst way to respond is by feeling sorry for yourself."

Ouch. Nobody likes to be told they are feeling sorry for themselves. Especially when it's true.

"When something doesn't go your way," Bud said, "when you lose, when you throw a pick, when you get passed over for a job—when you face disappointment of any kind—there are two ways most people respond.

"The first way is to feel sorry for yourself. You can get down on yourself or blame someone else for the misfortune. You can think, 'No matter what I do, things always go against me. What's the use in trying? Life's unfair. Poor, poor me.' You can lower your head as you walk around. You can shut yourself in and try to avoid seeing people. Any of this sounding familiar?"

I didn't reply.

"The second way to respond to a negative event is by doing everything you possibly can to change the situation," Bud said.

"Change it?" I said. "I can't go back in time and change the pass I threw."

"I didn't say anything about changing the past. I'm talking about changing the situation. The situation is you doubting whether you're good enough to be our quarterback. The situation is you feeling like a failure because of one pass. The situation is that our team needs a quarterback to be its leader in '88, but right now their QB is hiding out, skipping class, and walking around like a beat dog afraid to raise his head.

"That's the situation, Danny, and I'd say there's a lot you can do to change it. Don't you think?"

I shrugged.

"I didn't hear you," Bud said. He was losing his patience with my attitude.

"Yes, Coach," I said.

"The Arkansas game didn't end the way we wanted it to. Big deal. It's over and done with. It's in the past. I've moved onto next year's games and I need you to move on with me. As far as I'm concerned, it's a new year. Time to start fresh and focus on what's next.

"People who are insecure and loaded with self-doubt live in the past. They keep looking backwards. People who are confident are focused on the present and the future. They're always looking forward.

"If you don't like what happened in the past, then it's time to bust your ass making sure it doesn't happen again. The only way to do that is to focus on what's next. Right now, that means doing everything you can to prepare for next season.

"Stop looking backwards. Decide *right now* to turn things around. This is the only moment you have any control over."

There was urgency in Bud's voice. Though our next season didn't officially start for months, it had already started in his mind. He wasn't about to let himself or the team waste time wallowing in self-pity.

"I know what you're feeling," Bud said. "Everybody who has played this game or tried to do anything exceptional in life knows what it's like to fail. And I know it hurts. I know the memory is so fresh that you can't replace it with something else and it keeps you up at night thinking about it.

"There's only one solution and that's to focus all your attention on what you're doing right now and what you want to see happen in the future. Focus on lifting, running, studying—hell, even watching a movie or reading a book can take your mind off the past. You have to force yourself to be totally engaged in the current moment. Whatever you're doing right now, be in that moment. Don't get distracted. This is it. This is all you have. *This* moment. *Right now*.

"Because let me tell you, Danny, what you focus on right now will determine where you go in the future. What you did last week or last month or ten years ago doesn't mean a thing anymore.

"You can choose to look backward or look forward. The choice is yours. **The backward thinker will fall into insecurity and self-pity. The forward thinker will respond with confidence and a sense of empowerment.**

"You're at a crossroads, Danny. You've got two years left in this program. This is that time when players have to decide whether they're all in and focused on taking things to the next level or whether they decide their best days are behind them. Now is not the time to be passive and let someone else or some past mistake choose the path for you. You need to actively decide where you will go next."

The way Bud framed it as a crossroads moment added immediacy to the situation. Now was not the time to wait and see how long it would take me to get out of my funk.

Now was the time to get my butt in gear and *decide* to move forward.

"Too many people in this world respond to things not going their way by feeling sorry for themselves," Bud said. "That leads to feeling powerless and passive. **Champions respond by taking matters into their own hands and deciding they're going to do whatever it takes to change the situation.**

"It's time for you to respond like a man of action. It's time for you to respond like a champion. It's time for you to respond like the confident leader of this team."

A shift in perspective can be so powerful.

I had woken up that morning feeling like a failure — beating myself up for throwing the interception, blaming my parents for putting self-doubt in my head, blaming God for "making" me fail, telling myself that I just wasn't worthy of success. These were all passive, fatalistic perspectives.

Bud made me recognize the power was in *this moment*, not in the past. I could either be a passive, backward-looking person or an active, forward-looking person. Was I going to focus on the past or the future?

It's easy to dwell on disappointments in the past and reach the point where you disregard everything you could be doing *right this moment* to change your future for the better. Visualizing myself at a crossroads with the choice to take either the backward path or the forward path made it easier for me to snap out of my funk. I couldn't stand still and wait. I had to choose which direction to go.

Just before I left the film room that day, Bud added one more thing.

"Oh, and by the way," he said as I got up to leave. "Just so we're crystal clear. You skip another class this year and you're off the team."

"Got it, Coach. Won't happen again."

And it didn't.

22

"I don't think anything is unrealistic if you believe you can do it."

– Mike Ditka, Super Bowl Champion Coach and Player

1988

Seeing myself at a crossroads worked well for me. Whenever I thought about the interception I threw to end the 1987 season, I immediately called up the image of myself at an intersection where I could choose which way to go. I had the choice to move left or right. One direction represented the dark and shady past; the other direction represented a bright and sunny future.

I envisioned myself choosing the path towards the future and it snapped me out of self-pity mode. Seeing myself take a step on the bright path forward gave me a feeling of empowerment — a feeling that I was in control of my destiny.

This visualization technique helped me attack the

offseason with renewed confidence. I hit the weights hard and shaved one-tenth of a second off my 40-yard dash time.

Jerry Miller graduated, Mike Pederson decided to transfer, and I went through the spring as the starting QB. Though redshirt freshman Reggie Coleman was on my heels, I still had a better command of the offense.

I was gaining confidence with each lift, each practice, and each new day. The whole team was.

This confidence made me feel better about myself, which positively affected my personal life. Sherry and I started hanging out more and soon we realized we were dating again. It was great to have my best friend back.

Everything seemed to be looking up for me...except in one area of my life.

In April, Bud called me into his office and surprised me with a conversation that had nothing to do with my play on the field.

Bud was looking over a stack of papers on his desk. "Danny, I'm looking at your grades and I don't like what I see."

"You brought me in here to talk about my schoolwork?" I said. "Don't I have academic advisors for that?"

Bud ignored my questions. "You're a bright kid, but you're barely hanging onto a C average. You're underachieving. I don't care whether it's on the field, in the classroom, or later in your career, when I see one of my players not living up to his potential, it drives me crazy.

You want to tell me what's going on?"

"I, uh, I don't know. I guess I need to study harder."

"Don't give me that. What's the real deal here? I see you're taking the bare minimum hours each semester and skating by. In fact, it looks like you're retaking two classes this semester that you dropped last year. You need to graduate in two years and that's not going to happen if you keep doing this.

"I also see you've changed your major several times and right now you're majoring in management. What do you want to be after college?"

"I want to go into business," I said.

"What kind of business?"

I shrugged. "I don't know for sure. I envision myself with a desk job somewhere. Work my way up to the top of the company someday. That sort of thing."

"Sounds like a vague plan," Bud said, now making eye contact with me. "Do you have a passion for business?"

I chuckled. "I wouldn't say I'm passionate about it. But I want to make a good living after college. This route seems like the smartest way to do that. Get a business degree, then find a good company to work for. I've got two years to figure it out. I'm sure I'll find something I like."

"I don't think that's a wise approach," Bud said. "**People who succeed at a high level are those who have a strong passion for what they're doing**. Just like the best football players are usually the guys most passionate about football, the best business leaders, salespeople, teachers, doctors, lawyers, writers, or any other profession are those who are the most passionate about their fields. **Passion breeds confidence and energy.** You need to find a career that gets you fired up and excited. Something that gets you as excited and passionate as you are about football."

I shrugged again, not sure where Bud was going with this. "If there is such a career, I haven't heard of it."

"C'mon, Danny, I don't believe that. You're in college, you've got countless opportunities in front of you. If you could be anything when you're done being a football player, what would you want to be?"

"Anything at all?"

"Anything. What would be a dream career for you?"

I leaned back and thought about it. A smile crept across my face.

"I'd take Keith Jackson's job if someone was offering it," I said, laughing at the preposterous idea. Keith Jackson was a famous broadcaster who called many of the nation's biggest televised sporting events. There had to be thousands of people who dreamed of having his job.

"I could see that," Bud said.

I stopped laughing and raised my eyebrows at Bud. "Seriously?"

"You've got a broadcaster's voice," he said. "And there is an outstanding broadcast journalism program here at A&M."

"Coach, do you know how many people would love to have a job like that? I was joking around."

"Do you know how many people would love to be the starting quarterback at a Division 1 college? You're doing that, aren't you?"

I hadn't thought about it that way. In an instant, the notion of choosing a career that didn't feel like a job—something I was *passionate* about and would *love* to do each day—became more realistic to me.

"My point is," Bud said, "somebody's got to do it, *why not you*?"

I got lost in my thoughts for a moment, dreaming about a career where I got paid to talk about sports. How fun that would be.

"Do me a favor," Bud said. "Meet with the School of Journalism this week and look into it. You've got to find something you're passionate about, something that excites you. When you find it, I've got a feeling your grades will rise right along with your enthusiasm."

I did as Bud advised. My meeting with the School of Journalism led to several more. I read up on what a career in sports broadcasting would entail. The more I learned, the more excited I got.

In May, I changed my major and I started taking journalism classes that summer to catch up. Today, I'm living my dream of working in sports radio. I get to spend my days talking sports *for a living*. I can't believe how lucky

I am to have a job I enjoy so much.

It all started with that seed of inspiration Bud planted in me.

Why not me?

Somebody's got to have a career like that. Why not me?

Asking myself, "Why not me?" again and again built up my confidence as I navigated a highly-competitive career. There was no good reason I couldn't achieve this dream if I chased it with the same level of passion I chased football with.

I *could* make a living in sports broadcasting. Many others have. Why not me? All I needed was the training, the commitment, and the confidence that I could do it.

I would learn that just like with football, there are three components to any profession: the physical, the mental, and the psychological. The physical would involve putting in the long hours and the effort to get good at the job. The mental would mean studying the profession and learning what to do and when to do it. And just as Bud had taught us, the psychological was where I could separate myself from the competition...with confidence.

As with any other worthy goal, the biggest hurdle is usually believing you can do it. Once you have the confidence that you *can* do it, it feels like nothing can stop you.

23

"When you believe in yourself and the people you surround yourself with, you will win something really big someday."

– Dick Vermeil, Super Bowl Champion Coach

The big news of the offseason heading into 1988 was the recruiting class Bud signed. The media ranked it near the middle of the Southwest Conference and declared it the most impressive haul any coach had brought to Arkansas A&M since the school had joined the SWC.

The top recruit in the class was a running back out of Dallas named Clarence Washington. He was one of the top running backs in the state of Texas and it shocked the region when he chose us over all the other SWC schools. We couldn't wait for the highly-touted running back to join our team in August.

Bud also signed two quarterbacks, which was of particular interest to me. While I expected Bud to restock at the quarterback position after our roster had dwindled to just me, redshirt freshman Reggie Coleman, and a walk-on at the QB spots, I was anxious to learn more about the new players who would soon be competing for my position. I had to admit, I was glad to see that neither of the new quarterbacks were highly-rated recruits.

For the first time in decades, there was an optimistic buzz around town about Arkansas A&M football.

The excitement was contagious. Our offseason workouts were more energetic than any I had experienced before. No longer were guys quitting the team. No longer were there cynics in the corner of the weight room rolling their eyes at Coach Stonebreaker's enthusiasm. No longer were there players complaining about this or that in the cafeteria. There was an intense focus on the season ahead.

The culture of the program was changing. The negative guys who refused to buy in had been weeded out. Everyone who stayed was excited about where we were going and, despite the pain of our grueling workouts, we looked forward to going to work with each other every morning. The sacrificing together formed a tight bond within our team.

It's easier to be confident and excited about the future when everyone around you is feeling the same way. I guess that's what Bud meant when he would tell us, "**If you surround yourself with good and positive people, good and positive things will happen.**"

When the incoming freshmen arrived a week before two-a-day practices, I couldn't help but notice they too seemed to be a more enthusiastic group than previous freshman classes. Sure, they were still freshmen and they had the nervousness that comes with being introduced to a new environment away from home. But, as a whole, the guys seemed *happy* to be here.

That was not the case when I arrived at A&M.

Years later, I had dinner with Bud one night and asked him about his recruiting philosophy. He told me something I have never forgotten.

"That first year, the real recruiting comes in rooting out the people who don't want to be there," Bud said. "I didn't come in and kick anyone off the team because I believe everyone deserves a shot. But the ones who won't fit in stand out pretty quickly and they tend to weed themselves out. The key is to not be tempted to convince a player who isn't a good fit to stay just because he's talented. **A supremely-talented player with a negative attitude will do far more damage to a program than a less-talented player with a great attitude. You can't build your team with negative people and expect positive results. They will bring everyone down.**

"I took the same approach to recruiting new players. I always looked beyond talent alone. I wanted guys with the right attitude. Guys who would fit in with the positive environment I wanted to build. I wanted guys who loved football and who would build others up. I didn't want guys who complained and tried to pull others down. I don't like to work with people who aren't enjoying themselves and I know players don't either. Finding the right type of guys was never an exact science, but I had a good feel for the type of people I wanted to bring in. I knew how important it was to build the team with confident, can-do people.

"**You become just like the people you surround yourself with.** This goes well beyond football. **Your people create your culture and no organization will succeed for long if it's overrun by toxic individuals.**

"Surround yourself with negative people who complain, whine, and undermine, and you'll become just like them. You'll start making excuses and looking at the downside of everything. Any success you have will be short-lived and you won't have much fun along the way.

"On the other hand, if you surround yourself with people who are confident and positive and who enjoy going to work every day, you'll become just like them. Together, you'll all have a lot more success and a lot more fun.

"**Never underestimate the power you have in choosing who you surround yourself with and who you look up to.**

"**If the most important decision you make is deciding how you choose to see yourself, the next most important decision is deciding who you want to surround yourself with.** These are two decisions we're all constantly making.

"Choose wisely who you surround yourself with."

24

"I'm a firm believer in goal setting. Step by step. I can't see any other way of accomplishing anything."

– Michael Jordan, 6-Time NBA Champion and 14-Time NBA All-Star

The Sunday night before the first practice of the 1988 season, we had a team meeting. We were all itching to get started the next morning. I had a strange combination of excitement for what the new season would hold, but also a large dose of anxiety knowing I was about to do something extremely taxing both physically and mentally. Two-a-day practices may have been better under Bud than the previous staff, but they were still the hardest part of every football season.

"Tomorrow, we officially begin the new season," Bud said from the stage at the front of our meeting room. "Before we get started, I want to talk to you all about goals.

"First off, you must understand that **humans are designed to be goal-striving people. No person can truly be happy if he or she is not striving for a goal.** Goals give us our purpose.

"**If you ever find yourself feeling down or lacking energy, it's because you don't have any goals that excite you. Find a goal you're excited about and you will become an energetic person.**

"We need goals. We thrive on goals. Goals give us energy.

"Psychologists have discovered that when you make the conscious decision to set a goal, you plant that goal in your subconscious mind, which then goes to work doing everything it can to achieve that goal. Your subconscious is *constantly* working to achieve the goals you give it—even when you're not aware of it.

"The goals you set affect *everything* you do. When you set a goal and commit yourself to it, it will affect the way you think, talk, and act. Even when you're sleeping, your subconscious works to find ways to achieve the goals you've given it. That's the awesome power of goal-setting.

"You need to set goals for every area of your life. You need to set goals for what you personally want to achieve in the weight room, in the classroom, and on the football field. You also need to set goals for life outside of college. You need financial goals, spiritual goals, health goals, family goals, and career goals. You need to set goals for the type of person you want to become.

"Goals have a huge impact on your self-image. The size of your goals and the excitement they generate directly affect the way you see yourself. **A person with big, audacious goals sees himself as a big, attack-life type of person. A person with small goals sees himself as a small, feeble person.**

"You've got to have goals if you want to be successful and happy. A person without goals is a person without direction. A person without goals tends to be passive and insecure. He lets life happen to him instead of going out and creating the life he wants to live. He doubts his own abilities and he's afraid to set big goals because he's afraid he might fail. That's the sign of a person with a brittle ego, someone who doesn't think highly of himself.

"Tell me your goals and I can tell you what type of person you are.

"If you tell me you don't know what your goals are, that tells me you're too apathetic about life. If you tell me your goals are small things that any average Joe can accomplish, that tells me you're insecure and loaded with self-doubt.

"But, if you tell me your goals are big things — things that other people say are unrealistic or require too much work — then that tells me you're a confident person destined to be a winner in life. That tells me you're worthy of being an Arkansas A&M Bulldog."

"Damn right!" Brian shouted out. A few others clapped their approval.

"The confident person isn't afraid to set big, crazy goals," Bud said. "The moment you set a goal, it instantly triggers your mind into believing it can be achieved. **Whatever goal you give your subconscious mind, it will go to work trying to achieve it. The bigger your goals, the more confident you will become and the more efficient you will become at achieving those goals.**

"And just as every great person needs to set big, exciting goals in order to thrive and be happy, so does this team.

"Fellas, it's time to establish that one big goal that we will all be gunning for this season. A goal that will unite us all. A specific goal that we will all be focused on day and night from here on out. It's time to give your mind that one giant goal that is going to drive us through the season.

"That goal is a bowl game."

I heard some claps and hollers from my teammates.

"I'll be honest with you," Bud said, "heading into last season I really wasn't sure what to expect. I wasn't sure how many of you were ready to buy into the culture we're building. I wasn't gonna stand up here and announce a big goal for the season until I knew you were ready for it."

Bud looked around the room, cracked a smile, and said, "You are ready now. You are ready to take the next step."

More players, including me, cheered their approval.

"This program last went to a bowl game in 1961," Bud said. "That's twenty-seven years ago. *Twenty-seven.* If everyone on this team is committed — *fully* committed — to making it to a bowl game, I have no doubt you will be the team that ends that bowl drought. You *will* make history."

More cheers.

"Last year," Bud continued, "it took almost half a season before this team started believing in itself. This year, we're coming out of the gate strong. You're already miles ahead of where this program was last year at this time. Your confidence level is higher, your enthusiasm is higher, and this team is bigger, stronger, and faster than it was a year ago. You're ready to go bowling. You've earned the right to set this goal.

"It's time to send a message to those teams that have been sitting at the top of the Southwest. We're here to take one of their bowl spots. Let's see how they like staying home in December or January."

That line got everyone cheering.

"A bowl game or bust," Bud said. "That's our goal for this season. Who is with me?"

More cheers. The anxiety about starting practice the next day was giving way to pure excitement. I couldn't wait to get started.

Bud nodded his approval. "Our goal is a bowl game in '88. That goal will drive everything we do. I want you to think about that goal and see it coming to fruition. Feed that goal into your mind over and over. When you go to bed at night, take time to think about this goal, see yourself at a bowl game. Let that goal be the fuel that pushes you through two-a-days, through every practice, and through every game.

"When you're in pain, when you gasping for air, when you're sweating and bleeding and you don't think you can run another sprint or deliver another block, that's when you have to remind yourself why you're doing this. That's when you have to remember where you're headed. That's when you have to see yourself playing in a bowl game at the end of the year. **Visualizing where you want to end up will energize you and push you through your toughest moments.**

"But, here's an important key. When you remind yourself of the long-term goal, you must also remind yourself of what it's going to take *right this moment* to achieve that goal. When you wake up in the morning, I want you asking yourself, 'What do I need to do *today* to make this goal a reality at the end of the season? What's the next step? What do I need to do right now to make this happen?'

"Big goals are accomplished step-by-step. It's like climbing a tall ladder and each rung represents a step. You have to focus on the current step. If you start trying to skip ahead four or five steps, you're gonna fall off that ladder.

"Remind yourself again and again that all you have is this moment and it's what you do *right now* that will determine where you end up five months from now.

"Bowl games aren't earned in November. They're earned at every practice. It's the incremental daily goals that add up to achieving the big, long-term goals you're excited about.

"**You have to win today before you can win tomorrow.** You have to win this week and the week after that before you can win your first game. You have to win this moment before you can worry about the next.

"Focus on winning each day and then stacking those winning days on top of each other. If we keep stacking up winning days, we will eventually achieve our biggest goals.

"See yourself as a bowl worthy team and then ask yourself, 'What kind of effort do I have to put forward today to earn that bowl worthiness? What kind of effort do I have to give on this drill or this play? What kind of focus do I need to have in order to earn a bowl game over all those other teams that want one?'

"And fellas, let me level with you. We're gonna face adversity this season. There are gonna be ups and downs throughout the year. That's football. That's life. Don't get down on yourself and start thinking you've missed your shot because of a few bumps in the road. If you start feeling frustrated, remember your big goal. Remind yourself what you need to do *right this moment* to get there.

"Tomorrow, when we officially kick off this season, focus on what you must do during this practice, this play, this moment." Bud paused and let his words linger in the silence of the room. "Tomorrow, we start earning our bowl game!"

We all shot up and cheered. We started two-a-days the

next day more fired up than ever before.

25

"People must have confidence in themselves before they can realize their full potential."

– Mike Krzyzewski, 5-Time National Champion Basketball Coach

Our 1988 preseason camp began on one of those famously hot and humid dog days of summer in Arkansas. At 8 a.m., the temperature was already in the eighties and the sticky air served as a warning that we would soon be practicing in 100-degree heat. That didn't stop Bud from running out to midfield and greeting us as he always did.

"What a perfect day for football," he said. "It's a great day to be a Bulldog!"

And so began a preseason camp that was physically harder than anything I had ever been through before. The coaches were demanding more of us. They kept reminding us that right this moment we were competing with 104 other teams for one of those precious bowl spots.

The freshman quarterbacks Bud recruited were both faster and quicker than the QBs I was used to competing with and Reggie Coleman, now a redshirt freshman, was also competing for the starting job when camp began.

Coleman was an amazing athlete, probably the fastest guy on our team. He would wow us all when he found just a little open space and could take off like a rocket scorching down the field.

A few things kept him from taking the starting QB job. Too often, he would keep the ball on the option when he should have handed it off or pitched it. He still didn't look comfortable with the passing game and threw a lot of interceptions. And finally, he suffered a few injuries — nothing major, but enough that he'd have to leave practice early or miss a full day here and there, which hampered his progress. He hadn't quite figured out how to position his body to avoid taking big shots when running through the trenches as an option QB and his lean frame left him more vulnerable to injury.

During the third week of preseason camp, the coaches moved Coleman to wide receiver.

"We've got to find ways to get you the ball in open space, Reggie," Bud said one afternoon. "And if we can't get you enough space at QB, we're gonna have to do it at receiver."

Coleman was a natural at receiver. By the end of camp, he had officially changed positions and was rotating in regularly at his new spot.

That move was another confidence-booster for me. It

told me I was doing well enough at QB for the coaches to feel comfortable moving one of our best athletes to another position.

But that wasn't the biggest story coming out of camp. The biggest story revolved around our new halfback.

When I first saw freshman Clarence Washington, I thought he might be too small to excel at this level. He was just 5-foot-8 and maybe 190 pounds. But when I saw him carry the ball, I knew he was going to be a game-changer. He had all the ingredients you want in a running back: speed, balance, quickness, vision, and strength. He had a way of finding holes, cutting on a dime, and surging through defenses. Once he found daylight, he had another gear that allowed him to outrun most defenders. When he needed to, he could lower his shoulder and power through tacklers.

Clarence was going to be special. I could tell immediately. Everyone could.

With Brian leading the defense, me leading the offense, Clarence manning one of the halfback positions, and Reggie making big plays at receiver, our confidence as a team grew each day. Our young offensive and defensive lines also made strides with each practice.

By the time we got to our first game, we believed we were a bowl worthy team — and we couldn't wait to show the rest of the nation.

We started the year with a convincing victory over

Kansas, 31-7. The next week, we beat Sam Houston State (a Division 1-AA opponent), 51-13. It was the first time in twenty-four years that Arkansas A&M had scored more than fifty points in a game.

I rushed for a pair of short-yardage touchdowns against Sam Houston State and hit Reggie for a long touchdown pass against Kansas. Other than that, I wasn't doing much to stand out, but I was feeling comfortable running the offense.

Clarence Washington quickly caught people's attention as the freshman rushed for more than 100 yards in both of our first two games.

In week three, we ran into the Oklahoma State Cowboys and a running back named Barry Sanders. To this day, I've never personally witnessed a better running back than Sanders. He would rush for more than 2,600 yards in 1988 and win the Heisman Trophy.

We trailed the Cowboys, 38-21, heading into the fourth quarter and I tried to force some long passes into coverage late in the game. I ended up throwing two costly interceptions in the final quarter. We lost, 45-28. Oklahoma State would finish the year 10-2 and ranked No. 11 nationally.

After the game, Bud was quick to remind me that I had to move on. He wouldn't allow me to dwell on the picks I threw.

"The most important game of the season is always the

next one," he said. "We'll go to the film, we'll address our mistakes, but then we'll move on."

I wasn't the only person Bud was having these types of conversations with. Brian took the loss to Oklahoma State especially hard, feeling as though he was responsible for letting the eventual Heisman Trophy-winner zig and zag his way to nearly 300 yards rushing. Brian met with Bud Sunday morning and by Monday he was refocused on what we had to do next. Bud was teaching all of us how to bounce back from mistakes and rebuild our confidence.

We began Southwest Conference play with back-to-back close wins against Baylor and Texas Tech. By this point in the season, Coleman had worked his way into the starting spot at receiver and Washington was proving to be one of the most exciting freshmen in the SWC. Our team was starting to generate buzz.

We were 4-1 and talk of a bowl game was spreading beyond the walls of our team facilities.

That's when we hit the trouble Bud had warned us about prior to the season.

26

"Confidence is contagious, and so is lack of confidence."

– Vince Lombardi, 5-Time NFL Champion Coach

In our sixth game of the season, we lost to Texas A&M by ten points. We played hard against a team that would finish the year second in the SWC. Though we came up short, we knew we had gained this perennial power's respect. It was the game after Texas A&M that threatened to derail our season.

In a back-and-forth shootout against Houston and their run-and-shoot offense, the Cougars scored a touchdown with less than two minutes left in the game to take a 41-38 lead. We failed to pick up a first down on our final drive and Houston ran out the clock to defeat us.

We were devastated. I rushed for 112 yards and completed ten of my seventeen pass attempts, but my red-zone fumble recovered by Houston late in the third quarter and my failure to complete a pass on our final drive had me beating myself up again.

After all the optimism we had going into the '88 season, we were now 4-3 with SWC powers Texas and Arkansas still on the schedule. In a matter of two weeks, our goal of making it to a bowl game suddenly became a lot less likely.

We went into a bye week feeling like someone had let the air out of our tires. We were flat in practice and you could feel the momentum slipping away. I was trying to stay focused on the current moment, but I was playing tight again, so worried about making a mistake that I was hesitating on my option reads and pass deliveries. This, of course, led to more mistakes.

During a particularly gloomy afternoon practice, I watched Brian plead with the defense to show some energy.

"What's the matter with everybody?" a red-faced Brian shouted through gritted teeth. "Where's the passion? Where's the energy? Where's the big hit? Is this how a bowl team plays defense?"

He was desperately trying to light a spark, reminding his squad that the season was not lost and to practice like a bowl-worthy team. The defense responded on the next play with a big hit against one of our running backs and they celebrated as though they had just won the game with a goal-line stand.

After the way Brian called out the defense, Bud called me out.

"You see how Brian Dawson got the defense going

today?" Bud said to me after practice. He had pulled me aside on the way to the locker room. Now, just he and I stood out in the rain on our soggy practice field.

"Yes, Coach," I said.

"That's what leaders do. And that's what I need you to do. This offense needs a positive leader and I need you to step into that role."

Though my confidence had been building over the last two seasons, I still didn't see myself as a so-called *leader*. Who was I to encourage someone else to play with more purpose and focus when I was the one fumbling the ball late in the game? Who was I to pump someone up when I'm the one who needed extra motivation? I wasn't an all-conference player like Brian and I wasn't some highly-touted recruit. I was an average option quarterback, a placeholder until one of the younger, more talented, recruits picked up the offense.

Despite the progress I had made building a more a confident self-image, that was how I saw myself. I was grateful to be the starting QB and I felt confident I could run the offense, but a team leader I was not.

"I'm not really one of those rah-rah kind of guys," I said to Bud. "I never have been. I don't have a big personality like Brian."

"I'm not asking you to change who you are," Bud said. "Brian has his ways and you have yours. What I'm asking you to do is understand that—whether you want to be or not—as the quarterback you are leading the offense. They're looking to you for guidance. They're watching how you carry yourself and how you respond to adversity. You're out there saying the right things, but the way you carry yourself is just as important."

"What am I doing wrong?"

"Winston Churchill once said, **'Success is going from failure to failure with no loss of enthusiasm.'** Think about that. Does that describe you? Are you carrying yourself that way?"

I lowered my eyes. "I'm not feeling particularly enthusiastic today. When I look at my teammates, I can see I've let them down. They don't see me as a leader; they see me as the guy who keeps losing the game for everybody."

"That's not true at all," Bud said. "They're responding to how you see yourself. The way you see yourself is spreading throughout the team.

"Let me ask you something. What's the first thing that comes to your mind when you think of a guy like Terry Bradshaw?"

"Bradshaw?" I asked, unsure what a retired NFL quarterback had to do with me and this team. "Four Super Bowls."

Terry Bradshaw had led the Pittsburgh Steelers to four Super Bowl victories from 1974 to 1979. At the time, no other team had won four Super Bowls and no other quarterback had gone 4-0 in the biggest game on the planet.

"Four Super Bowls and two Super Bowl MVPs, right?" Bud said.

I nodded.

"No quarterback has ever performed better in the biggest game of the year. Is that fair to say?"

I nodded again. In the fall of 1988, Joe Montana had only won two of his four Super Bowls and Tom Brady was just eleven years old. Terry Bradshaw's Super Bowl legacy was unmatched at the time.

"Well, did you know that in his first Super Bowl victory, he passed for less than one hundred yards?"

"Seriously?"

"Seriously. And did you know that in his second Super Bowl victory, he threw more incomplete passes than complete passes?"

I shook my head. I didn't think it was possible to win a Super Bowl completing less than half of your passes.

"Yet, he led his team to a come-from-behind victory in the fourth quarter of that game," Bud said. "Everyone remembers the sixty-four-yard touchdown pass he threw to Lynn Swann. Nobody remembers that Terry had a forty-seven-percent completion percentage that day."

"If he ended up winning two Super Bowl MVPs, then he must have stepped his game up after those first two Super Bowls," I said.

"Yes, he did. He passed for more than three hundred yards in each of his next two Super Bowls. And that's what people remember. His victories, his MVPs, his leadership, his cannon arm, his touchdown passes. You know what a lot of people forget? The three interceptions he threw in his final Super Bowl."

"I do remember that," I said, remembering an NFL Films documentary on Super Bowl XIV. "He threw three picks, but still led the Steelers to a fourth-quarter comeback for the win."

"That's right. He was named Super Bowl MVP despite throwing three picks. He won the game and the MVP award because of the way he bounced back from his mistakes.

"Are you seeing a pattern here? The man with the perfect Super Bowl record was far from perfect in those games. He threw too many interceptions, he missed a lot of passes, he made a lot of mistakes. Yet, he also led his team to epic fourth-quarter comebacks.

"At the end of the day, Terry Bradshaw was great at the most important thing: bouncing back from adversity. He didn't lose his confidence. He kept his enthusiasm. He never believed he was out of the game and that rubbed off on his teammates. They never stopped believing in him because he never stopped believing in himself. They knew he could make mistakes, but they also knew he would bounce back from those mistakes. They saw it in his eyes. They saw it in how he carried himself.

"You can't act like you just lost the game every time you

make a mistake and you can't act like the season is a disaster when we lose a game. You have to have a bounce-back attitude. You have to stay confident and enthusiastic no matter what kind of adversity you're going through.

"**Having a positive self-image means being secure enough in yourself to know you can make a mistake and still be successful.** It means going from one disappointment to the next with no loss of enthusiasm. It means knowing that yes, there are going to be failures, but in the end you will come out successful.

"Don't let self-doubt creep in every time something doesn't go your way. **It's not about whether or not you make mistakes, it's about how you bounce back from them.** A bounce-back attitude starts with how you carry yourself.

"**You have to act confident in order to be confident.** Stand tall. Move with a purpose. Don't cower. When adversity strikes, make yourself bigger, not smaller.

"The way you carry yourself spreads to everyone else. Vince Lombardi said, **'Confidence is contagious. So is a lack of confidence.'** If you carry yourself with confidence, it will not only make you feel more confident, but that confidence will spread to others.

"You are responsible for how you carry yourself and that is not a responsibility you can take lightly. Your attitude affects everyone around you."

"How do I force myself to be confident when I feel bad

about myself?" I said.

"You use the methods we've talked about. Change the channel on negative memories. Talk yourself up and *decide* to be confident. Envision yourself at a crossroads and *choose* the path forward. Relentlessly focus on *this* moment and the *next* opportunity. Think about your goals.

"There's also something called the modeling method. It's a simple, but powerful technique. You **ask yourself, 'How would a confident leader respond to this situation?'** How would Terry Bradshaw, a four-time Super Bowl winner, respond to a turnover? How would Joe Montana respond to throwing a pick? How would Walter Payton respond to fumbling the football?

"**Keep a confident role model in your mind and then emulate what they would do. The more you try to act confident and self-assured, the more confident and self-assured you will be.**

"Think of some confident people. Think of how they perform under pressure. Think of how they react to adversity. They can be athletes, business people, even actors in movies. Just give your mind someone who exemplifies confidence."

Bud and I talked about people who personified confidence and I came up with several more as I thought about it later. I thought of people from various professions who projected confidence. I thought of the huge action stars of the time—how did they carry themselves in their movies when faced with adversity? I thought of recent concerts I had attended, seeing Bruce Springsteen and Van Halen performing with nonstop energy in front of huge crowds—what was it about the way they carried themselves that exuded such enthusiasm for life? I thought of successful coaches of the era like Mike Ditka and Barry Switzer—they didn't lower their heads and cower into a corner when something went wrong in a game. I thought of a few basketball stars like Larry Bird, Magic Johnson, and a young, new phenom named Michael Jordan—how did those guys react to missed shots?

Envisioning their body language in response to high-pressure situations or disappointments gave my mind an image to emulate. As I tried to copy their body language, I stood a little taller, spoke with more conviction, and carried myself with more confidence.

The more I acted as I envisioned a confident person acting, the more confident I *became*. The physical triggered the mental.

That confidence became contagious and spread throughout the team just as Bud knew it would.

27

"In the face of adversity, you find out if you're a fighter or a quitter. It's all about getting up after you've been knocked down."
– Archie Griffin, 2-Time Heisman Trophy Winner

By the time we played Texas in 1988 — a team that started the year ranked No. 3 in the nation — we had put our back-to-back losses behind us and were focused on proving we were a bowl-worthy team. Led by Clarence's season-high 156 yards rushing, we avenged the previous year's lopsided loss with a hard-fought 21-14 victory.

It was the first time Arkansas A&M had defeated the Longhorns since joining the Southwest Conference and though Texas would end up having an uncharacteristic losing record by the end of the year, it was a pivotal moment for our program. We were finally showing that we could beat the "blue bloods" of the SWC.

After the win against Texas, we beat Rice in convincing fashion and then beat TCU by a touchdown. That brought our overall record to 7-3 as we entered our final game of the regular season against undefeated Arkansas.

For four quarters, we battled it out with the eleventh-ranked Razorbacks and never quit, but in the end, they outmuscled us and pulled away with a 31-10 victory. They played us much tougher than they had the previous season — almost like we had woken up the sleeping bear by playing them close the year before.

We walked off the field frustrated by yet another loss to our in-state foes — our program's twenty-first consecutive loss to Arkansas.

As for my personal performance, I went a forgettable four-for-fourteen passing while rushing for just twenty-nine yards on twelve carries. I also fumbled the ball twice. It was my weakest performance of the season. I don't know if I was intimidated by Arkansas or overwhelmed by their talent (probably a little of both), but the Razorbacks brought out the worst in me.

Arkansas keyed on Clarence all day and held him in check. Reggie Coleman was open a few times on pass plays, but I missed him with overthrows early and underthrows late. Our offense never got into any kind of rhythm and we played from behind all day. I was unable to break a big play when we needed it, either rushing or passing.

The Razorbacks were playing on another level. I left the field wondering if we'd ever be able to beat them.

28

"The most important thing to do for our children, our athletes, and anybody else is to get them to believe in themselves – to get them to raise their self-confidence and their self-image."

– Lou Holtz, National Champion Football Coach

The loss to Arkansas left us with a 7-4 record and a fourth-place finish in the Southwest Conference. While we were proud to have a winning record and a place in the top half of the SWC, none of us were celebrating much. We had one big goal coming into the season and that was a bowl game. We didn't know if our record was strong enough to make that dream a reality.

We had to wait a full week after our regular-season finale to find out if we would be invited to a bowl game. The Sunday after Thanksgiving, a team meeting was called.

Bud took the stage of our meeting room, looked over his anxious audience, and let a smile slowly creep across his face.

"Fellas," he said, "we've been invited to the Liberty

Bowl."

The room erupted with cheers.

"I take it you all accept that invitation." he shouted above the joyful chaos.

All the hard work we had put in. All the confidence we had worked to build. All the believing that we were a bowl-worthy team. It had all paid off.

I'll never forget the hugs and the sheer joy we felt that afternoon. People nowadays may not realize how big a bowl game invitation was back then, especially for a program that had struggled so badly for so long. I saw tears in the eyes of coaches, players, trainers, and administrators who were in the room during the announcement.

That night, I was so excited I could barely sleep. I couldn't believe how far this team had come in the two seasons since Bud arrived.

I also thought about how far I had come as a person. I was no longer the scared, timid, self-doubting, self-pitying person I had been two years ago. I believed in myself. I believed in my teammates. I believed in Bud Sullivan and the coaching staff that mentored us. I believed in the power of self-confidence.

How could I not? I now had clear, undeniable evidence proving what an impact a person's self-image can have on performance. The Arkansas A&M Bulldogs had gone from the bottom of the SWC to the Liberty Bowl.

The night Bud arrived at this school, I kept asking

myself, *What if Bud Sullivan is right?* I had asked myself that question again and again as I contemplated whether to quit the team.

That question had been answered emphatically.

A few weeks later, we went to Memphis and won the Liberty Bowl. I spent most of the night handing off or pitching the ball to Clarence (who, by the way, was named the Southwest Conference's Newcomer of the Year after rushing for more than 700 yards during the 1988 regular season—a school record for a freshman).

Clarence rushed for 139 yards and three touchdowns in the Liberty Bowl. I passed the ball just three times, completing two of them (both to Reggie), and ran the ball seven times for twenty-eight yards.

The victory gave us a final record of 8-4 and we finished the season just outside the national rankings.

Arkansas A&M had come a long way in two seasons, but Bud had a much bigger vision for the future of the program.

29

"If you're going to be a championship team, you have to think championship thoughts."

– Pat Riley, 5-Time NBA Champion Coach

1989

At our first team meeting of 1989, Bud announced the bar was being raised.

"Over the past two years," Bud said from the podium, "I've seen you all grow from men who didn't think they deserved to win a game to men who believed they deserved a bowl game. That's awesome. I'm proud of you all for buying in, believing in yourselves, and believing in each other. I'm proud of the hard work and enthusiasm you've brought to the weight room and the practice field. That got you to where you are.

"Now it's time to take the next step. Make no doubt about it, our goal is not to make it to just any bowl game in 1989. Our goal is to go to the Cotton Bowl. And to do that, we must win the Southwest Conference. Nothing less than the conference *championship* is the goal this year.

"I believe you can do this. I believe this team is ready. It's going to take a lot of hard work. It's going to take a lot of mental toughness. It's going to take a lot of confidence, enthusiasm, and sacrifice to make this goal a reality. But I believe we can do it. I would not set a goal I didn't one hundred percent believe we could accomplish.

"The time is now, fellas. It's time to go beyond seeing yourself as a winner and to start seeing yourself as a champion.

"To make that shift, everyone on this team must think bigger and work harder than ever before. Like everything else, it's a choice you make. It's up to you. Are you ready to start thinking like *champions*?"

We now had a giant new goal driving us through our offseason workouts. Bud, Coach Stonebreaker, and the rest of the staff were constantly encouraging us to see ourselves as champions worthy of being the very best in the conference.

They challenged us with questions like, "Is that how a champion acts? Is that how a champion talks? Is the effort you're giving enough to be the very best in the Southwest? Is that the attitude of a champion?"

In hindsight, I see that Bud waited until he knew we were ready to set a goal this big for the team. If he had come in during his first season and told us our goal was to win the Southwest Conference, none of us would have believed him. We could barely envision winning a SWC *game*, let alone winning the entire conference. We would have lost faith in him after losing our first few SWC games.

Bud had earned our trust after two seasons of progress. Now, when he told us we were capable of winning the conference, we believed him.

30

"There are three things we can't have: We can't have complacency; we can't have selfishness; and we can't lose our accountability. ... When you're arrogant, it makes you complacent and it creates a blatant disregard for doing things right."

– Nick Saban, 7-Time National Champion Football Coach

Bud hit the recruiting trail hard and by the time Signing Day in 1989 arrived, all the newspapers and recruiting services were raving about the class he signed. Across the board, they ranked his recruiting class as one of the top two in the Southwest Conference.

This was all very exciting for everyone in the program, but I must admit that noticing Bud had landed a top-rated quarterback named Michael Murray made me wonder what kind of competition I'd soon be facing for my job as the starter. I tried not to think about it much and spent the winter and spring months focused on doing everything I could to win a SWC championship.

During the Sunday night meetings leading up to the '89 season, Bud continued to teach us invaluable life lessons. His main emphasis during the offseason was on growing, never getting complacent, and rising to the next level of competition.

"A confident person is not arrogant," Bud said one Sunday night. "An arrogant person thinks he knows it all. He doesn't think he needs to keep improving. That's how arrogance leads to complacency. **A confident person is never complacent.**

"**You can't rest on your past achievements. You have to keep moving forward. If you think you've arrived and that you're now** *entitled* **to something, you're setting yourself up for defeat.**

"You can be and should be proud of your accomplishments, but as soon as you think you no longer need to improve—that's the moment you lose your ambition and become complacent. Complacency is one of the worst things that can happen to a person. **If you don't have that drive and enthusiasm to always get better, you're gonna get beat by somebody who does.**

"Don't ever allow yourself to get complacent or arrogant. Understand that you'll never know it all. Be secure enough to realize that there is always more to learn and always room for improvement.

"Some people never ask for help or advice because of their ego—they think it makes them look weak. Don't be that guy. Never stop growing and learning."

Another Sunday night, Bud talked to us about the danger of comparing yourself to others. This spoke to me not only because I couldn't help comparing myself to the other quarterbacks in our conference, but also because I knew a blue-chip QB would soon be arriving to compete for my job.

"**A confident person doesn't focus on what anybody else is doing,**" Bud said. "**A confident person focuses on doing everything he can do to be the best he can be. That's it. That's his focus.**

"**Worrying about what somebody else is doing is a sign of insecurity. Comparing yourself to others is a sign of insecurity.** One of the fastest ways to decrease your confidence level is to start obsessing about the things others have that you don't.

"Focus only on what you can control: *your* effort and *your* attitude.

"Don't waste time and energy comparing yourself to others. If you keep your focus only on becoming the very best *you* can be, things will end up working out for you on the football field and everywhere else in life.

"I'm not asking you to completely ignore the competition. I'm asking you to understand the purpose of competition. The people you compete with, the other teams you go up against—all they represent is a measuring stick. They are there to push you, to help you grow, but that's it.

Don't be intimidated or distracted by them. Keep your focus on what *you* can do to make *yourself* better.

"You can't control what others are doing. All you can control is what *you're* doing. The moment you start worrying about what somebody else is achieving and how that compares to you is the moment you give away your power.

"Insecure people are obsessed with what others are thinking and doing and how that compares to them. Confident people are too busy working on becoming the best they can be. They recognize that we're all unique individuals with specific God-given talents, interests, and abilities. No two people are alike. And that's a good thing! Your only job is to become the very best that you can be; to become the person *you* were born to be."

On other Sunday nights, Bud would hammer home principles we couldn't be reminded of often enough.

"You're the only person who can give yourself confidence," Bud said. "I can't give it to you. Nobody else can, either. Don't blame me or anyone else for how you're choosing to feel about yourself. You're the one who must decide to be confident. You're the one who must see yourself as a leader. I can't crown you with those things. You have to give it to yourself by taking charge of how you think."

I loved those Sunday night meetings. The lessons I learned had a lifelong impact on the way I saw myself and the world around me.

Off the field, I was becoming a more confident and positive person, which led to just about everything else in my life going great in the spring of '89.

In school, I was excited about my new major and I was learning everything I could about the world of broadcasting.

At that time in the late '80s, a newish radio format known as "sports talk" was growing in popularity. These were radio shows where the hosts talked nothing but sports while interviewing sports personalities and taking questions from callers. It seemed like a dream job to me. The more I learned about it, the more I wanted to make it my career.

The more passionate I became about this field of study, the better I did in class and my grades rose steadily.

Things were also going great with Sherry. I proposed to her in the summer. She accepted and we set a date to get married the following summer, after we graduated.

Heading into my senior year, I felt like everything was going my way.

That is, until preseason camp began.

31

"Do you want to play it safe and be good or do you want to take a chance and be great?"

– Jimmy Johnson, Winner of 2 Super Bowls and 1 National Title

I was excited to kick off the 1989 season. We all were. There was an aura of confidence surrounding us, a feeling that this year would be special.

"This is our year," Brian Dawson kept shouting throughout practices. It became our theme. This was the year we would take the step nobody thought was possible. This was the year we would complete the worst-to-first turnaround. This was the year we would become *champions* of the Southwest Conference — an idea that seemed ludicrous just three short seasons ago.

This was the year. It had to be.

For seniors like me and Brian, this was our final season, our final shot at making history at Arkansas A&M.

To take the next step as a program, Bud decided to change our offense from a three-back wishbone formation to a two-back I-formation.

On the one hand, this change made perfect sense. We had one of the best young running backs in the conference and being able to feature Clarence as the one, primary tailback would give him more carries. Plus, changing to a two-back offense would give us more of a passing threat so teams couldn't keep loading the box and keying so much on our running game. This was how many option offenses were evolving at the time. Nebraska was building a dynasty running the option out of the I-formation and Notre Dame had just won the 1988 National Championship with a quarterback who could run the option and still pass the ball often enough to give defenses fits.

On the other hand, I didn't like the change because expanding the playbook and opening up the offense meant more passing plays (not my strong suit) and new reads that I would have to master.

"Are you sure it's a good idea to change the offense?" I asked Bud one afternoon in the film room when I was frustrated with learning the new system. "I thought the wishbone was working."

"We're still going to be an option team," Bud said. "But football, like life, is ever-changing. Teams are adapting to what we're doing, so we've got to adapt right back. Those great defenses we've been facing at Arkansas and Texas A&M have been stacking the box and shutting us down. We've got to adapt and make them cover more field. Plus, I like the idea of getting Clarence more carries and Reggie more catches."

I didn't argue with him. Teams like Arkansas had pretty much shut down our rushing attack the last two seasons and we had no answer. We needed more of a deep threat to keep defenses honest. I nodded and told Bud I agreed, but my memories of throwing interceptions when I went deep were seared into my mind. The truth was, I was afraid to throw the ball downfield and I think Bud knew it.

My junior season had been better in terms of limiting mistakes and making smarter decisions, but I only broke a few big plays. I was pretty good at grinding out a few yards on the option when the team needed it and I was better at hitting short and intermediate passes. What I lacked were those exciting touchdown runs late in the game or that deep pass when the team needed a big play.

I had become what football analysts refer to as "a game manager." I could manage the game well enough to not blow it against average competition, but could I take this team to the next level — the championship level?

It didn't help my confidence when Michael Murray arrived on campus. He was the top recruit in the class Bud signed and though he was only a freshman, it was evident right away that he was a tremendous talent. Not only did he have the speed and athleticism to excel at running the ball, but he also had a cannon for an arm. He could throw beautiful downfield passes.

I sensed the excitement surrounding him. This kid was going to be amazing. But starting as a true freshman would be a tall order. In practice, he made some jaw-dropping runs and throws, but he also had some fumbles, some misreads, and some ugly interceptions. He had the raw talent, but he needed to learn the offense and adjust to the speed of defenses at this level.

As advised by Bud, I tried to focus on only what I could control—playing the best that *I* could play. During our preseason practices, I focused on playing smart and sound football. I was more deliberate with my option reads and I consciously chose to throw to receivers on shorter, higher-percentage routes instead of risking the deep ball. I wanted it to be indisputable that I was the safe and reliable choice as the starting quarterback.

A week before our opening game against Louisiana Tech, Bud posted the team depth chart and I was still the starter. I was relieved, but not complacent. I could see the progress Murray was making and I knew it would only be a matter of time before he made a serious challenge for the starting job.

Though I felt my plan to focus on being safe and reliable at QB was working, Bud was not satisfied with the way I had been playing during camp. He called me into his office and let me know exactly why.

"You're playing too safe," he said. "And it's holding you back from playing great. To be great, you've got to be willing to go big. Yes, you're making good reads and you're protecting the football — these things are important. But you're also passing up too many opportunities because you're afraid to make a mistake. You're afraid to let loose.

"In our scrimmages, you've kept the ball less and less on the option — even though you've had lanes open up for you. There have also been several times where you've avoided throwing the deep ball to open receivers in favor of shorter routes. When you play it too safe it costs us points. If we're going to take the next step as a team and win a championship, I need you thinking bigger. I need you to take some chances when they're there."

"You want me to be more reckless?" I asked.

"No, never reckless. I want you to be opportunistic. I want you to be confident in your ability. You've got the speed and athleticism to go up against any quarterback in this conference. I can see that; you need to see it too. You've also got a more accurate arm than you give yourself credit for.

"**Don't be afraid to take chances when you're presented with great opportunities. You can play it safe and be good or you can take a chance and be great.** As a team, we have to think bigger. Confident people aren't afraid to think big and take risks. If we're going to be a championship team, we need a quarterback who is willing to aim bigger, not smaller."

"I can do that," I said. And I meant it. Bud was giving

me permission to think bigger. He was telling me I could do the very things I was afraid to do. I trusted him.

"I know you can," he said. "You're not the self-doubting kid you were two years ago. You're a confident leader with the talent to take us to the Cotton Bowl. But you've got to unleash that talent. You've got to unleash the greatness within you. The only way to do that is to let loose and just play. Stop overanalyzing everything. Stop comparing yourself to anyone else. Don't be so worried about making a mistake. **Have the confidence to trust yourself and trust your ability.**

"You've worked your whole life for the opportunity in front of you. Don't squander it by thinking small.

"Remember how I told you that at some point a person must simply *decide* to be more confident? And then, as you choose to be more confident, your confidence will grow and you'll play better?"

"Yes," I said.

"In the same way, **a time comes when a man must stop waiting and hoping to be the man he wants to be and he must start** *being* **the man he wants to be. You must** *decide* **to trust yourself.** Remind yourself of all the hard work and training you've put in to earn the opportunity in front of you. Remind yourself of all the failures you've learned from and all the obstacles you've overcome to get to where you are. And then, trust yourself and seize the moment.

"To be great, you have to have the confidence and

courage to take bigger shots. Holding back and hoping that someone else makes a mistake is a recipe for mediocrity. To achieve greatness, you've got to take risks and trust yourself.

"Yes, you will make mistakes. Yes, you will fail. But I know you can bounce back from any mistake you make, just as you have always done in the past.

"**Stop worrying so much about what will happen if you swing big and miss and start focusing on what will happen if you swing big and connect.** Forgive the baseball analogy, but that, Danny, is the difference between home runs and walks.

"You'll never know what you're capable of if you don't take a chance and see what you've got. I'm giving you permission to take some chances. Show me what that looks like. I trust you. I need you to trust yourself."

This was another one of those lessons from Bud that applied to life beyond football.

Ten years after I graduated from Arkansas A&M, I was working as the sports director for the news radio station in Joline. I was broadcasting local high school games and also working as an analyst for A&M football and basketball games. For two years, I had also been hosting a two-hour nightly sports talk show. The pay wasn't great, but it was stable and I loved what I was doing.

That's when I was presented with a unique opportunity. I heard about a group in Kansas City launching a new twenty-four-hour sports radio station. I sent my samples, I interviewed, and I was offered the job—a chance to host a daily sports talk show.

It was an outstanding opportunity, but the risk was high.

Sherry had just given birth to our third child and she was staying home with the baby. Because the station was just starting out, the new job would pay me less than I was making in Joline and it was less stable. The Joline station had a long history and was the only news radio station in town. At the time, there was still uncertainty regarding which markets could sustain round-the-clock sports radio stations. More than a few sports talk stations across the nation had shut down after trying the format. There was no guarantee this new Kansas City station would fare any better.

I faced a tough decision. The Kansas City station was offering me the chance to have my own show in a bigger market. If the station and my show were successful, it would lead to even bigger opportunities. But initially it meant lower pay, greater risk, and a move to a new city where I would be working with all new people.

That's when I remembered Bud's guidance about not being afraid to take risks. I called up my old head coach and asked for his advice.

We discussed what my biggest goals were and compared how the job I was being offered and the job I currently held either helped or hindered those goals. When I told him my dream was to someday host my own nationally-syndicated sports talk show, he told me exactly what I expected, "Do you want to play it safe or do you want to take a shot at making your biggest dreams come true? **All big dreams require big risks. To achieve greatness, you've got to accept that risk and believe in your heart that you can overcome any obstacles it may bring.**"

I took the leap and accepted the job in Kansas City. Within five years, the station had become hugely popular and I was hosting the top-rated show. Four years after that, I took another big risk and started my own nationally-syndicated show. Today, *The Dan O'Connor Show* is one of the most-listened-to sports talk shows in the nation.

None of it would have happened if Bud Sullivan had not taught me that great achievements require taking risks that most people won't take. He taught me to be courageous and take the necessary risks in order to make my biggest dream come true.

He taught me not to settle for anything less than what I really wanted out of life.

32

"More often than not, it's the expectation of success that defines championship teams. ... What you believe and what you expect have a tendency to come about. Those who have positive expectations experience positive results more often than those who have negative expectations."

– Tony Dungy, Super Bowl Champion Coach and Player

After my meeting with Bud in the summer of '89, I was different at practice. He had given me permission to let loose and, yes, fail. But fail forward. He knew I could not become the quarterback I was capable of becoming if I was not willing to take some chances.

Our conversation made me realize I had not been playing to win at practice; I had been playing not to lose my starting job. Truth be told, I had been playing that way for most of the '88 season as well.

The last week of August 1989 was the best week of practice I can ever remember having. Yes, I threw some picks. Yes, I took some big hits and even fumbled once during a scrimmage. Yes, I missed my receivers on a few deep shots. But, I also felt faster and lighter than I had all summer. I broke several big touchdown runs during the week and completed more passes of twenty yards or more than I ever had in one week of practice.

Despite some setbacks here and there, I was trusting myself and I could sense my confidence rubbing off on the rest of the team. We were ready to make a championship run.

The college football preview magazines heading into 1989 gave us plenty of positive press.

Athlon's wrote: "If you haven't noticed, the Arkansas A&M Bulldogs are no longer the cellar-dwellers of the Southwest Conference. Last year's 8-4 season has put the rest of the conference on notice."

Lindy's wrote: "A Liberty Bowl victory last season has expectations rising at Arkansas A&M. With the recruiting classes Bud Sullivan is bringing in, the winning season in '88 is not likely to be a one-time fluke."

Sports Illustrated and *The Sporting News* both listed Bud as one of America's top "coaches on the rise."

However, along with the positive press came a recurring sentiment that almost every magazine shared: Arkansas A&M is still a year or two away from competing for the conference title. The media agreed we were heading in the right direction, but not strong enough to take the next step. The preseason magazines unanimously ranked Arkansas,

Texas A&M, and Houston as the top teams in the Southwest Conference and ranked us near the middle of the pack.

Our first game was at home against Louisiana Tech. Though not quite a sellout, I read that it was the largest season-opening crowd in more than twenty years at Arkansas A&M. I ran for two short touchdowns in the first half and completed a 46-yard pass to Reggie Coleman on a crucial third down early in the game. But the story of the day was Clarence Washington's 203 yards rushing. We won the game, 37-10.

We followed that up with a 48-6 win against Kansas. I passed for 216 yards and three touchdowns, the most passing yards and TDs I had ever thrown for in one game.

To be fair, Kansas was a struggling program and Louisiana Tech had just made the move up to Division 1-A. We were expected to have lopsided wins those first two weeks. Our first real test would be against a ranked Texas A&M team to open up conference play.

After our team dinner the Friday night before the Texas A&M game, Bud gave us another memorable talk.

"I want to talk to you about the power of expectations," he said. "The older I get, the more I realize that **the expectations you have for yourself tend to come true**. It's crazy how dependably it happens. **Life tends to hand you pretty much what you expect it to.** Sure, there are surprises here and there, but the way you see yourself — what you expect to become when you get older, the career you expect to have, the family life you expect to have—it all tends to become reality.

"Something to be aware of is that you may not realize exactly what it is you're expecting for yourself. You might subconsciously expect to emulate the life your parents have lived, which can be good or bad depending on how they chose to live their lives. You might be expecting something negative without realizing it. Somebody might have told you that once all the fun and excitement of your college football career is over, life will be a drag. Somebody might have told you that all you're good for is playing football. You might be expecting those comments to come true.

"I want you all to do some soul-searching and make sure you're rooting out any negative expectations you might have for yourself. This is one of the most important things I'll ever teach you.

"Your expectations tend to become reality, so make sure you set positive expectations for yourself.

"This goes for football as well.

"To achieve the goal we set at the start of the season, you must not only believe you *can* be the best team in the conference, you must *expect* to be the best. You must expect positive results. You must expect to win.

"When you expect to be the best team on the field, your actions will follow your expectations. You will play up to your expectations.

"**When you expect to achieve something big, you hold**

yourself to a higher standard. When you perform up to that standard, you end up achieving exactly what you expect. You live up — or down — to the standard you expect of yourself.

"Fellas, Texas A&M is ranked number twenty in the nation. Our program hasn't defeated a single ranked team since joining the Southwest Conference. Tomorrow, I *expect* that to change."

We cheered our approval.

"No longer are we expecting to be anything less than a great team. No longer are we expecting to be anything less than the best damn football team in this conference!"

More cheers.

"If we expect to be the best, then we expect to beat everybody in this conference. Ranked, not ranked, it doesn't matter. We expect to be the best team on the field. Come tomorrow afternoon, we're going to start living up to those expectations!"

More cheers and claps. We were getting pumped up. Bud waited for us to quiet down and then continued.

"When you go to bed tonight," he said, "I want you thinking about what you expect of yourself. I want you to keep repeating to yourself, 'I expect to play the very best game I have ever played. I expect to win. I expect to be a champion.'

"As you repeat those lines, visualize those expectations becoming reality. See yourself performing exactly as you expect to perform. Don't dwell on mistakes, failures, and defeats. When those thoughts creep into your mind, see yourself overcoming them. Blast them away with positive expectations. Focus on succeeding. **What you feed your mind matters and what you focus on most tends to come about.**

"When you declare your expectations and visualize them playing out, you are feeding your subconscious mind the specific expectations you have for yourself. Your mind then goes to work to make sure those expectations become reality.

"That's the power of expectations. Don't take this power lightly. Not in your career, not in your family life, and not on the football field.

"I'll say it again, what you expect for yourself tends to become reality. Make sure you're expecting only positive things for yourself.

"And that starts with expecting to be the best team on the football field tomorrow afternoon!"

Once again, the dining hall erupted with cheers and we couldn't wait to take the field on Saturday.

33

"If you're going to take gambles, you must have one thing: self-confidence."

– Don Shula, 2-Time Super Bowl Champion Coach

For three quarters, the Texas A&M game was a defensive slugfest. Neither team could get anything going on offense. The Aggies loaded the box and keyed on Clarence. Led by Brian, our defense stymied their offense as well. It was scoreless at the half and tied, 3-3, at the end of the third quarter.

Just before the fourth quarter was set to begin, Bud put a hand on my shoulder pads, pulled me close, and said, "Danny, we're not going to win this thing by playing it safe. It's time to take some shots. It's time to trust yourself. I trust you and so does everyone else on this team."

His words were like a jolt of confidence. I nodded with focused eyes. I believed I was ready to lead this team through the air.

He called an option pass play where I take two steps just

as I would on a normal option play, but then back up and look to pass the ball downfield. We had tried the same play early in the first quarter, but I overthrew an open receiver. Bud thought the time was right to try it again.

Sure enough, their defensive backs were playing tight and keying on the run. As their cornerback rushed towards the line of scrimmage to stop the option, Reggie blew past him before the defender realized it was a pass play. I let it fly and this time hit Reggie in stride. He went untouched for a sixty-yard touchdown.

Texas A&M answered with a long drive and tied the game, 10-10.

Bud called for more pass plays on our next drive. I knew we weren't going to catch the Aggies sleeping on the pass this time. Their secondary was ready for me to throw the ball and I had to take some shots into tighter coverage. I nearly threw two interceptions on the drive, but my receivers helped deflect the ball to the ground. If either of those passes had been picked off, it would have given Texas A&M good field position and could have cost us the game.

Those near-interceptions didn't stop Bud from calling more pass plays. He saw something he wanted to exploit through the air. He trusted me to come through.

On second-and-four at midfield—an obvious running situation for an option team like ours—Bud called for a play-action pass. I rolled out to throw the ball and saw my fullback open in the flats five yards down the field—an easy pass to complete. But I also saw one of our receivers running a deep post through the middle of the field with a step on his man — a more difficult pass, but a bigger reward if I could complete it. I went for the deep ball. I chucked an imperfect pass that was a little behind my receiver. He came back for it as the defensive back caught up with him. The two arrived at the ball simultaneously and after a brief bobble of the ball, my receiver fell to the ground with the ball in his hands at the seventeen-yard line.

Three plays later, we ran a play-action bootleg to the right and I hit my tight end in the endzone for the go-ahead touchdown.

We won the game, 17-10.

To the shock of everyone in the stadium, we won with two fourth-quarter touchdown *passes*.

In the offseason, Bud had told us that in order to take the next step we would need to be a passing threat in big games. He said we would have to stretch the field and not rely so much on the run when great defenses stacked the box. He said we would have to think bigger and take more risks.

Against Texas A&M, we lived up to the expectations Bud had been setting all offseason. The risks paid off and resulted in our program's first win over a ranked opponent since joining the Southwest Conference.

34

"To be an overachiever you have to be an over-believer."

– Dabo Swinney, 2-Time National Champion Football Coach

The win against Texas A&M propelled us to a 3-0 record and a No. 25 national ranking. It was the first time our school had been ranked since the 1950s. There was an exciting buzz all around town. Practices were intense. We felt good about ourselves. We *expected* to win.

And win we did.

We won our next five SWC games. Clarence Washington was averaging more than 100 rushing yards a game while I was averaging around fifty yards a game on the ground and more than 100 yards passing. My stats weren't big compared to what dual-threat quarterbacks put up these days, but back then, for an option team like ours, my numbers were pretty good. As I got more comfortable passing the ball, defenses had to respect our passing ability, which therefore made our running game even more effective.

It was incredible how far our program had come in just three seasons. We were now 8-0 and ranked No. 14 in the nation. We were playing in front of sellout crowds at home, we stood atop the SWC standings as the only team in the conference still undefeated, we beat Texas for a second-straight season, Brian Dawson was named a finalist for the Butkus Award (which goes to the nation's top linebacker), and Bud Sullivan was being called one of the top coaches in the nation for the fast turnaround he had engineered.

The culture surrounding our program had completely changed.

I had completely changed.

I had gone from being afraid to take the field to becoming the starting quarterback for a top-fifteen team. I had gone from nearly quitting on my dreams to chasing those dreams with everything I had and sincerely believing they could become reality. I had transformed from an insecure, timid kid to a confident, outgoing man. I believed in myself. I saw myself as a winner, someone worthy of success.

I was far from the only one who had gone through this transformation under the guidance of Bud Sullivan.

Our team had gone from a kicked-around group of perennial losers, whiners, and excuse-makers who lacked self-confidence to a nationally-ranked football team expecting to win every time we stepped on the field. With each game, we gained more confidence. When we took the field, we had the type of self-assurance great teams have.

"What about the danger of overconfidence?" I asked Bud one day after practice as we walked back to the locker room. "I never hear you talk about that. Growing up, I feared being *too* confident, like I might jinx myself if I have too much confidence."

Bud stopped walking and gave me a smile. "That's a great question. I never talk about overconfidence because I've never seen a team lose because it was *too* confident. Too complacent? Yes. Too arrogant? Yes. Too lazy, unfocused, or undisciplined? Yes, yes, yes. But not too confident.

"I think overconfidence is a misunderstood term. What people are really talking about is arrogance and complacency. If a player is always bragging and telling everyone how great he is, he's trying to hide his insecurity. If a player thinks he's so good that he doesn't have to put in the work anymore, he's about to get beat. The confident man isn't delusional; he knows he's always got more to learn and room to improve. Remember, confidence *requires* hard work and preparation. That's how you earn confidence. **If you haven't put in the work, you don't deserve to be confident.** And you'll know that deep down. You'll know whether you've earned the right to be confident."

I nodded, remembering all the times Bud had stressed that exact point over the last three years.

"As for jinxing yourself," Bud said, "that's nonsense.

You underperform when you doubt yourself, not when you believe in yourself. *Never* **stop believing in yourself.** As long as you put in the work and preparation, you can never have too much confidence."

Our team was proof of that. We were playing at the highest level in the history of the program. We believed in ourselves. We expected to be champions.

Of course, the season wasn't over. We still had three regular season games to go and our biggest challenges were ahead of us.

35

"Confidence is not, unfortunately, something you own forever once you've found it. It's something you must constantly work on."

– Dr. Bob Rotella, World-Renowned Sports Psychologist

One of the most important lessons I learned from Bud is that your self-image is something you have to *constantly* work on. There is no quick fix that ensures you will never doubt yourself again. Building confidence is an ongoing, lifelong process.

On the first Saturday of November in 1989, we had a rare late-season nonconference game. And it was a big one.

The Florida State Seminoles were an independent team back in those days. They were also one of the nation's top programs. They started the '89 season with two-straight losses, but rebounded with six consecutive wins including an upset win over No. 2 Miami the previous week. The Seminoles were now ranked No. 6 in the nation.

Florida State had blown us out, 45-14, just two seasons

ago. But we were a new team now. Everybody in our locker room believed that.

In a matchup billed as the biggest game ever played in Joline, Arkansas, I felt confident when we took the field for warmups, but immediately noticed how much swagger the 'Noles came out of their locker room with prior to the game. They were big, strong, and fast. Our sellout crowd did not intimidate them. They were here to take care of business.

Florida State got the ball first and the Seminoles drove down the field in just six plays to take a 7-0 lead. They had incredible speed at the receiver spots and their quarterback was precise with his passes.

When I took the field down 7-0, for the first time in 1989 I was...intimidated. I walked up to the line of scrimmage with doubt creeping in. *These guys are out of our league*, I thought to myself as I looked over their daunting defense shifting around with pre-snap adjustments. Their defense was loaded with fast and powerful future NFL players. Seeing their defense on film, I was impressed, but not intimidated. Seeing them in person was another story.

On the first play, I handed the ball to Clarence for a run up the middle and a wall of Seminoles collapsed down and met him at the line of scrimmage. They yelled and pounded into each other celebrating the impressive first stop of the game. Even the way they celebrated was intimidating.

On the next play, I ran an option to the right and tried to stretch it out, but by the time I was forced to pitch the ball to Clarence, Florida State was there to push him out of bounds for a loss of two yards.

On third down, we called a pass play. I panicked as my offensive line got pushed towards me and I threw an ugly pass that sailed over the head of my intended receiver.

Three-and-out just like that. A poor punt gave the Seminole offense good field position and two plays later they scored another touchdown.

From that point on, everyone in the stadium knew it was going to be a long day for the Arkansas A&M Bulldogs.

By halftime, we trailed 24-0 and I had completed just two-of-nine pass attempts with one interception. Our running game had also been held in check.

On the first drive of the third quarter, I took a hard shot near the sidelines and landed awkwardly on my shoulder. It was my non-throwing arm, but the trainers were concerned it might be dislocated. My day was done. They took me to the locker room and I have to admit that part of me was relieved to be leaving the field.

My shoulder was strained, not dislocated, but I still watched the rest of the game from the sidelines with my arm in a sling. We lost the game, 38-17.

Michael Murray, our highly-touted freshman quarterback, scored both of our touchdowns after coming in to replace me.

In the locker room after the game, Bud told us he was proud of our second-half performance. Nobody quit.

Still, we all felt dejected. We had been knocked down a few pegs from where we thought we were prior to the game.

Had we just been lucky up to this point? Were we benefiting from a schedule that was backloaded—easier at the start and more difficult at the end? Were we about to be exposed as the same old Arkansas A&M Bulldogs, the team that didn't belong anywhere near the top of the conference?

36

"I'll never let anyone talk me into not believing in myself."

– Muhammad Ali, 3-Time World Heavyweight Champion

The Sunday after the loss to Florida State, I read *The Joline Post* sports columnist's postgame article, which included this passage near the end:

"The bright spot of the afternoon was true freshman Michael Murray's second-half performance. Unintimidated by the 24-point deficit he inherited, the blue-chip quarterback commanded the offense with a quiet confidence not seen in the first half. In fact, Murray and the Bulldogs outscored the mighty Seminoles in the second half.

"In earlier games this season, we've seen flashes of Murray's outstanding potential in mop-up duty. On Saturday, we saw Murray against one of the top defenses in the nation and he didn't disappoint.

"With the Bulldogs' two biggest SWC games of the season still on the schedule, I believe it's time for a quarterback change."

There it was. An article publicly calling for my job.

While I knew Bulldog fans were anxious to see more of our highly-touted QB recruit, I had performed well enough in our first eight games to avoid a quarterback controversy. That was beginning to change. People were questioning whether I was worthy of the starting job.

So, this is the point where I once again lost my confidence, cowered into self-pity mode, and mentally checked out, right?

Wrong.

Not this time.

Bud's methods for building and *maintaining* self-confidence were becoming second-nature to me and I refused to let the Florida State game, or the call for me to be benched, knock me back into self-doubt.

I was no longer the insecure person I once was.

At this time, Brian and I were renting a house with a couple other players and I had my own bedroom. On Sunday night, I went into my bedroom, locked the door, closed my eyes, and blasted my mind with the confidence-building techniques Bud had taught me.

I reminded myself that all the mistakes I made on Saturday were lessons to learn from. Lessons to grow from. Just like learning lessons in class, it wasn't personal. Precisely *because* of those mistakes and the lessons they taught me, I would be a better quarterback going forward.

I told myself I was a hard worker. I reminded myself of all the strength and speed gains I had made in the weight room. I reminded myself of how prepared I was and how much I had learned studying endless hours of film. I was a fifth-year senior who had made giant strides in my mental, physical, and psychological abilities. I had earned the right to be here and I believed I was capable of leading this team to a conference championship.

I called up memories of some of my greatest moments as a quarterback. I recalled my game-winning touchdown pass against Texas A&M just a few weeks ago, my tackle-breaking runs, my perfectly-placed passes, my open-field speed. I played a mental highlight reel of my best plays dating all the way back to high school.

I thought of my biggest goals and reminded myself they were all still intact. We lost one game. It happens. We were still undefeated in conference play and on track to win the SWC. I envisioned myself playing in the Cotton Bowl, what an incredible experience that would be. Since I was a little kid, I had dreamed about playing in a major bowl game on New Year's Day. That dream was now within striking distance and just thinking about it flooded me with excitement.

I felt the passion for the sport I loved playing. I thought about the guys I played with, guys who were like brothers to me now. Guys like Brian and Clarence had become two of my closest friends and every Saturday we got to battle alongside one another. I refused to let the Florida State loss lessen my enthusiasm for the game I loved so much. I was getting to play major college football with my best friends. What could be more exciting than that?

I reminded myself that the past was the past and that what I did *next* would determine my future. It was another crossroads moment and right now, at this very moment, I chose to be confident and enthusiastic about what was *next*. I refused to go down the dark path of past disappointments.

I envisioned confident people I admired. I reminded myself what confidence looked like, how confident people carried themselves. I would emulate them. I would show that same kind of confidence to my teammates. They needed to know they could rely on me and I was going to present myself as the confident leader they could trust.

I refused to wish things were different. I refused to wish that a quarterback with Michael Murray's talent was on some other team. I chose to be thankful that Murray was on our team, pushing me to be a better quarterback. I chose to embrace the competition. I did not play my best game on Saturday, but I was getting better every time I took the field and the best was yet to come.

I would not allow a columnist's—or anyone else's—opinion affect my self-confidence. Instead, I would make sure I was following the three rules for building self-confidence: do the right thing, do everything to the best of my ability, and genuinely care about other people. If I followed those three rules, then it wouldn't matter what anyone else thought or said about me. I could feel good about myself because I knew I was following those three rules.

I would not *hope* that maybe I would play better next week. I decided that night I would *expect* to play better. I *knew* I would play better.

As these thoughts flooded my mind, I felt myself change mentally and physically. I walked out of my room a different person, standing taller and feeling stronger. The loss to Florida State was behind me. We were two games away from making our dream of winning the conference come true. *That* was my focus now.

Everything I had been through had led me to this point. Every obstacle, every failure, every seeming coincidence — it was all happening *for* me, not to me. I chose to believe that.

I chose to be confident. I chose to believe in myself.

I decided to become the man I wanted to be right that moment.

Bud had once said, "**The more you work on being confident, the more natural it becomes.**"

I was now experiencing exactly what he meant.

37

"Every team faces some kind of adversity. Mediocre teams are destroyed by it. Good teams survive it. Great teams get better because of it."

– Urban Meyer, 3-Time National Champion Football Coach

Starting with our Monday morning workout and all through the week, I made it a point to carry myself with confidence. I smiled a lot and talked about how I couldn't wait for this week's game. I hit the weights hard and I practiced hard. I offered encouraging words to anyone I saw with their head down.

My goal was to exude confidence to the team. I didn't want anyone thinking I was doubting myself.

I had always been more of a quiet person on and off the field, but the guys saw the passion in my eyes. They saw I had not lost my enthusiasm after the loss to Florida State. They realized I wasn't going anywhere. I had not lost my confidence.

As a team, we shook off the loss and responded with a

business-like mentality as we turned our focus to what was next: the No. 15 Houston Cougars.

With eventual Heisman Trophy winner Andre Ware quarterbacking their high-flying run-and-shoot offense, the Cougars were 6-2 and averaging more than fifty points a game. Though they had lost two SWC games — to Texas A&M and Arkansas — both losses were by less than a touchdown and could have easily gone the other way. Along with their high-scoring offense, they had a stout defense that held opponents to just fourteen points a game. There were many who felt that, despite the two losses, Houston was the most dangerous team in the conference.

If we could beat them, we would guarantee ourselves at least a share of the SWC title.

Facing a loud and raucous crowd in the old Houston Astrodome, I played what was statistically the greatest game of my career.

Our plan going in was to slow down the game with a clock-chewing option attack that would keep Houston's quick-striking offense sidelined as long as possible. Of course, things don't always go as planned. Teams must adapt to whatever happens. On this Saturday, what happened was a high-scoring, back-and-forth shootout.

Houston focused so much on stopping Clarence and our fullback that lanes opened up for me on our option plays. In the first half, I broke touchdown runs of sixty-one, forty-six, and thirty-two yards. In the second half, the Cougars made adjustments to stop me from running all over them and I passed for touchdowns of forty-five, sixty-five, and forty-three yards.

When the game was over, I had rushed for three touchdowns and 196 yards. I had passed for three touchdowns and 214 yards while completing better than eighty percent of my passes. That's six touchdowns and more than 400 yards of total offense. Easily, the most impressive numbers of my career.

The forty-three-yard touchdown pass I threw to Reggie with less than two minutes to play was probably the best-looking ball I've ever thrown. And it gave us a 49-47 lead.

But Houston came back, marched down the field with two fourth-down conversions, and kicked a field goal on the final play of the game to beat us, 50-49.

Despite playing what was the greatest statistical game of my career, our team fell short. Brian was sidelined with a bad ankle sprain early in the first quarter and was not allowed to return—despite begging the trainers to let him back in. He and I both watched helplessly from the sidelines as Houston's field goal split the uprights on the final play. We couldn't believe it.

The trip back to Joline was a somber one. Bud tried to pick us up, but even our eternally optimistic head coach had trouble finding the right words after such a gut-wrenching defeat.

The goal we set at the start of the year—winning the

SWC and going to the Cotton Bowl—was something we all believed in. We *expected* to achieve it. But after two consecutive losses, that goal was now in serious doubt.

38

"Do not allow negative thoughts to enter your mind for they are weeds that strangle confidence."

– Bruce Lee, Legendary Martial Artist

We had a bye week after the Houston game, which meant we would have two weeks to prepare for our final game of the regular season: a showdown with Arkansas.

The last-second loss to Houston was devastating and watching film of the game wasn't easy. I watched myself throw a couple off-target passes, make a few poor reads on the option, and stumble to the ground on a run I should have scored a touchdown on—these were opportunities that could have changed the outcome of the game, but I failed to capitalize on them. We all recognized missed opportunities that could have been difference-makers.

However, we remained confident. I know that sounds strange after two tough losses, but we still believed in ourselves. Bud had taught us well.

We looked back at the Houston game objectively and

saw that despite a few missed opportunities, we had played well overall—and we did so without the heart of our defense, Brian, on the field.

Bud told us, "That was one of those games where we didn't lose, we just ran out of time."

We believed him.

Yet, despite remaining confident as a team, something was off during our bye week of practices. With me, with Clarence, with Brian, with everybody. We were making uncharacteristic mistakes, turning the ball over, running the wrong routes, missing blocks. It was like we were regressing to a tight and fearful style of play.

After putting up the best numbers of my career against Houston, I was back to playing cautious. I saw Brian hesitating on defense—something he never did before. Reggie suddenly had a case of the drops at receiver.

What was the matter with us?

We were preparing for the biggest game of the season and the excitement should have been sky high. Instead, each practice only led to more frustration. It was as though momentum was gathering and pushing us in the *wrong* direction.

We could not afford to take a step back. Mighty Arkansas loomed and we knew how big, strong, and athletic they were. Breaking down their film, we didn't see many weaknesses. All week long we were reminded of how well the Razorbacks did this or that and how we would need to play an almost-perfect game to cancel out their strengths on both sides of the ball.

The more film we watched and the more we talked about them in practice, the better Arkansas got…in our minds.

The back-to-back losses knocked us to No. 23 in the national rankings. The Razorbacks were ranked No. 9. It would be the first-ever meeting between our two programs when both teams were ranked.

Thanks to a surprising mid-October loss to Texas, Arkansas had a 9-1 overall record and a 6-1 record in the conference. We had an 8-2 overall record and also a 6-1 conference record. The winner of our game would win the Southwest Conference.

For years, it seemed like Arkansas A&M always found a way to lose to the Razorbacks. Arkansas had a twenty-one-game winning streak against us and most of the games during that streak were lopsided. Even when the games were close, we always found a way to blow it at the end — like when I threw an interception in the end zone during the final minute of play two seasons ago.

Arkansas never wanted us in the Southwest Conference in the first place and they were determined to remind us we didn't belong every time we played them. Since joining the SWC, Arkansas A&M had never defeated Arkansas, losing by an average of more than 30 points a game in the series.

The Razorbacks represented everything that we were

not. They were the blue bloods of the state and a SWC perennial power; we were the state's "other" program and a SWC perennial cellar-dweller. They were the classy big brothers; we were the laughable little brothers. They had all the state's top players; we were where players landed if they couldn't play for Arkansas.

Those facts weren't helping our team's morale as the game drew closer. After two tough losses, the excitement around town had faded, too. It seemed like everyone was dreading what the Razorbacks might do to us.

To me, the problem wasn't a lack of confidence. I knew we were a good football team, we all did. We beat everyone in the conference except Houston—a team that beat us on a last-second field goal without Brian on the field for most of the game. We beat Texas, the team that accounted for Arkansas' lone loss. There was no reason to doubt ourselves as a team.

The problem wasn't apathy. We weren't tired from the grind of the season. We still had plenty left in the tank.

The problem wasn't complacency. We weren't satisfied. We wanted to be champions. We wanted to go to the Cotton Bowl.

But still, we were practicing poorly and the pressure was building. There was a sense of foreboding in the air.

By the end of the week, I recognized exactly what the problem was.

Fear.

I think we had all quietly hoped our dream of winning a SWC title wouldn't come down to the Arkansas game. History was stacked against us in the series. It was like we were cursed.

We were afraid of the mighty Razorbacks and it was showing by the way we practiced during the bye week.

I sensed it. Brian sensed it. Everyone sensed it.

Bud most definitely sensed it and when we started practice the Monday after the bye week, Bud was determined to squash that fear.

39

"Don't worry about losing. Think about winning."

~ Mike Krzyzewski, 5-Time National Champion Basketball Coach

On the Monday that would begin our final week of regular-season practices, temperatures hovered around forty degrees and an icy rain clacked against our helmets.

"What a perfect day for football," Bud said as he greeted us at midfield prior to practice. "It's a great day to be a Bulldog!"

Usually, that line got some enthusiastic cheers from the team. On this day, I heard only a few half-hearted claps. The mood of the team had not changed since the previous week. We were cold and wet as we stood on the soggy grass, still fearing the fate that awaited us on Saturday.

Bud wasn't deterred. He smiled at our weak reaction.

"I've said it before and I'll say it again, what you focus on tends to come about. That means when you focus on all the reasons why you should lose, you're probably gonna lose.

"You all spent last week focusing on big, bad Arkansas. How great they are. How they've beat us for twenty-one straight years. How they're the defending conference champs and we're not supposed to have a shot against them.

"I saw it in the way you practiced. Everybody was weighed down by fear. Everybody was nervous and nobody was having any fun. That's because you were focused on them and not us. You were focused on the obstacle and not the opportunity.

"Fellas, I believe **the size of the obstacle equals the size of the opportunity**. The bigger the obstacle in front of you, the bigger the opportunity you've been given."

Bud reached into his pocket, pulled out a silver coin, and held it up.

"Picture every looming situation as a coin," he said. "One side of the coin represents the obstacle and the other side represents the opportunity. The two sides are equal in size and weight. From a distance, the coin looks the exact same regardless of which side you look at. The coin itself doesn't change regardless of which side is up or which side is down. But when you get close and look at it, you see that the two sides are distinctly different."

Bud flipped the coin in the air and caught it. He opened his palm to reveal the coin. I was close enough to see that it was tails.

"If the coin lands on the obstacle side, that's all you will focus on," he said. "You'll keep looking at that obstacle until it's all you can think about. The more you look at it, the bigger the obstacle gets in your mind. At some point, you convince yourself there's no way you can overcome that obstacle.

"But the truth is, anytime you want, you can flip the coin over."

Bud flipped the coin to heads.

"Flip it over and what do you see?" he said. "Nothing but the opportunity. When all you're looking at is the opportunity, *that's* what you focus on. The more you focus on the opportunity, the bigger the opportunity gets in your mind. Eventually, all you can think about is the opportunity.

"Here's the key: you can't focus on two sides at the same time. You're either focusing on the obstacle or the opportunity. You can't see both. You're either envisioning everything that can go wrong or everything that can go right. All the reasons you can win or all the reasons you can lose. The side you focus on determines the side you're most likely to experience.

"I let you spend all of last week focusing on the obstacle side. It's time to flip that coin over. You've looked at the obstacle long enough, now I want you looking at the opportunity."

Bud put the coin back in his pocket and gave us a grin.

"On Saturday, we have the *greatest* opportunity in the

history of Arkansas A&M football," he said. "You will be playing for a conference championship and a trip to the Cotton Bowl. That's what is in front of you. That's the opportunity you have earned.

"You should be proud of yourselves for earning this opportunity. But, beating Arkansas and winning the conference isn't the only opportunity you should be thinking about. That's great if it happens. Don't get me wrong, we all want to win on Saturday. But the greater opportunity in front of you is the one you're experiencing right here, right now. Today. This moment.

"The season is winding down. We have this week and then the bowl game. That's it. I don't have to tell you seniors how quickly it all goes by and these final few weeks will be no exception.

"Don't waste it. Don't waste these final weeks together, playing the game you've loved your whole life. Don't waste it worrying about the obstacle ahead—I want you focused on the opportunity at hand.

"**One of the best ways to minimize the obstacle and maximize the opportunity is to focus on doing what needs to be done right now. Commit yourself fully to the task at hand and don't look too far ahead.**

"This is your moment. Your opportunity isn't off in the distance, it's right here in the present. You have the opportunity to spend these final weeks of the season doing something you love to do with people you love to be around — people who have become like family to you.

"Regardless of what happens in our final two games, what you're gonna remember most is how you spent your time together on these practice fields, in the weight room, in the locker rooms, hanging out with each other on the busses and planes. Enjoy these days. Don't waste them by fearing what might be ahead. Embrace them by being the best you can be and having fun here and now."

I noticed myself exhale. As the focus shifted away from our opponents — something we had no control over — to ourselves and only what we *could* control, I felt like I was unclenching for the first time in more than a week.

"I don't want you to look back," Bud said, "and remember these final weeks as a time when you were fearful and worried. I want you to be able to look back and know that you gave it everything you had — and you had a helluva lotta fun doing it!"

I clapped and others joined in.

Bud was nodding and smiling as he continued. "We're gonna have fun during these final practices of the season and we're gonna have fun playing Arkansas for the conference championship on Saturday.

"This game is very important to all of us. That's what makes it fun. It wouldn't be any fun to play a game you didn't care about. But don't make it so important that you can't enjoy it. Don't make the obstacle bigger than the opportunity.

"Football is just like life. When you try to achieve something important and difficult, you will face setbacks along the way. When that happens, regroup and choose to focus on the next play, the next game, and the next *opportunity*. That's the great thing about life — regardless of what happened on the last hand, you always get a new hand to play. There's always another opportunity. The secret is to enjoy and make the most of each of those opportunities *as they happen*. Never look back in regret or ahead in fear.

"**How you choose to view the world around you determines the type of world you experience**. How you choose to view the game of football — or any other aspect of life — determines exactly what you get out of it.

"You can choose to focus on the bad or the good. You can focus on the things you don't want to have happen or the things you do. You can focus on the obstacles or the opportunities in front of you.

"**When you focus on the obstacle, it makes you feel insecure and fearful. When you focus on the opportunity, it makes you feel confident and excited.**

"**Insecure people shrink away from the obstacle, but confident people step up to the opportunity.**"

Bud was not only giving us advice on how to win in football; he was giving us advice on how to win in life.

"I want you to loosen up and have fun out here." Bud's face turned intense. This was not an idea he was offering us; it was an order he expected us to follow. "Make the most of these final days together. Forget about *them*, focus on *us*! Focus on what makes *us* great, not them!"

We hollered our approval and started practice in a completely different state of mind than the one we had walked onto the practice field with.

Bud's talk set the tone for the new week of practice. All week long, he kept everything upbeat and his enthusiasm was contagious.

"One of the keys to having fun and enjoying the moment is to not even think about the results," Bud said one afternoon. "Instead, think about getting the most out of this moment. Find the joy right here, right now. Embrace it. Live in this moment and give it everything you've got. Do that and the final result will take care of itself."

Though Bud didn't want us getting so focused on results that we overlooked the current moment, he also kept reminding us to see ourselves as winners. He continuously shouted out confidence-building maxims in the week leading up to the Arkansas game.

"**You've got to believe it if you want to achieve it.** *Expect* to win every play."

"**You will never outperform your self-image.** See yourself as a champion. Play like a champion!"

"Nine times out of ten, the most confident team is gonna win."

"**Never underestimate the power of belief.** Believe in

yourself. Believe in this team. Believe that you deserve to be champions."

Bud also kept reminding us to have fun, loosen up, and enjoy these final days together. For seniors like me, the message carried particular weight: these would be my final days playing for Arkansas A&M. I would never again wear a Bulldog helmet after these last few weeks.

In fact, these would be my final days *ever* playing football. I would not have a pro career, as was the case for most the players on this team. These were my last days playing the game I had loved so much.

Bud's message was a wakeup call. I was not going to spend my final weeks worried and fearful, letting the pressure get the best of me. I was going to make the most of this time. I was going to enjoy this opportunity.

As the decades have passed, I've tried to embrace Bud's philosophy. Whenever times get tough or I feel overwhelmed, I remind myself to not take whatever it is I'm worried about so seriously. I remind myself to not sweat the small stuff and to find the joy in whatever moment I'm experiencing right now. I remind myself to focus on the opportunities more than the obstacles in my life.

It's not always easy. Some problems are bigger than others and I don't suddenly find myself without a care in the world. But trying to find the joy, reminding myself to play this hand out and that there will be a new hand dealt shortly, focusing on all the things I have to be grateful for —

these things always make me feel better.

As I start to feel happier, I feel more confident and I'm able to find solutions to whatever problem I'm working through.

I choose to enjoy my life. I choose to play the game of life to the best of my ability and to enjoy every moment I can.

40

"Human beings can accomplish almost anything if their minds tell them it can be done."

– Tony Dungy, Super Bowl Champion Coach and Player

In the days leading up to the Arkansas game, not only did Bud remind us to have fun and get the most out of the moment, but he and the rest of the coaches also chipped away at the invincible reputation so many of us had built up around the Razorbacks.

The coaches continuously reminded us of all the reasons why we *could* beat Arkansas. We had beat the same Texas team that beat Arkansas. We were faster or bigger or stronger or smarter at this or that position. The Razorbacks had never seen this play or faced this scheme. Over and over these examples were repeated.

"I believe with all my heart we're gonna shock these guys," Bud said at practice early in the week. "Just wait, they have no idea what's coming. We're gonna make history on Saturday and it's gonna be a blast."

He spoke with such conviction. You couldn't help but believe him.

Talk like this continued all week.

By Friday, no longer did we fear facing the Razorbacks. It was the opposite—we couldn't wait to take the field against them.

When Saturday arrived, the feeling was much different from our previous games against Arkansas. Even at their home stadium, we weren't tight and anxious. We were loose and excited. We felt like we had a little secret about how this day was going to go and the Razorbacks were in for a big surprise.

We were confident.

Bud told us before the game to enjoy the opportunity and to leave everything we had out on the field.

"Have no regrets," he said. "Don't worry about the score. Focus only on what you have to do dominate the current play. You do that and the results will take care of themselves. You've earned the right to be in this position, playing for a conference championship. Now, go out there and play like you *expect* to be champions."

At the coin toss prior to the game, the referee flipped the coin, I called "heads," and that was how it landed. I couldn't help but smile at the good omen—a reminder to focus on the *opportunity* in front of us.

What followed was one of the wildest football games ever played in the series—a classic game fans still talk about thirty years later.

Arkansas got the ball first and rode their option offense—an offense very similar to ours—down to inside our twenty-yard line. But the drive ended when they ran a play-action pass, trying to catch us overplaying the run. Brian read the play perfectly, didn't bite on the fake, and stepped in front of the pass for an interception at the twelve-yard line.

We drove down the field and kicked a field goal to take a 3-0 lead. Arkansas answered on the next drive to take a 7-3 lead. The game became a back-and-forth battle with our two teams trading the lead eight times through the first three-and-a-half quarters.

I made mistakes throughout the afternoon, but I bounced back quickly after each one. In the second quarter, I threw an interception on one drive, came back the next and threw a touchdown pass. In the third quarter, I fumbled on a third-and-one play, but on fourth down I broke a thirty-two-yard run for a touchdown.

No matter what happened, I refused to back down. For the first time in my college career, I wasn't intimidated by Arkansas. I saw myself as a worthy quarterback, capable of competing at their level. I belonged at this level. *We* belonged at this level. We saw ourselves as champions and we played like champions.

The back-and-forth classic would be decided in the final minute of play.

With fifty-four seconds left to play, we were trailing, 28-23. We had the ball at midfield. The situation was eerily similar to the one I faced just two seasons ago — when I threw an interception in the end zone that cost us the game.

I shook the memory from my mind. I refused to fear the same thing happening again. Instead, I saw this moment as an opportunity to rewrite a past mistake. I was a better, smarter quarterback than I was the last time I encountered this situation.

We drove down the field with mostly short, safe passes. Twice I went deep, and twice the ball fell incomplete — once an overthrow and once a broken-up pass that was nearly intercepted. Still, we stayed alive and kept moving the ball.

By the time we reached the Arkansas twelve-yard line, we were out of time outs with only nine seconds left to play. There was time for two plays max and we had to score a touchdown.

On first down, I dropped back to pass and saw zone coverage. Wisely, the Razorbacks were keeping everything in front of them. They didn't want to get beat to the end zone with man coverage.

I noticed Reggie on a post pattern heading for the middle of the field. He had a small window between defenders. I had to take a shot. I let it rip through the middle of the field.

Two defenders and Reggie converged on the ball at the goal line. The three bodies collided.

The ball fluttered into the air.

Their free safety dove for it.

The ball hit the turf an instant before he could secure it. Arkansas players celebrated as if he'd caught it, but the referee waved it incomplete. The Razorback fans booed their disapproval. I breathed a huge sigh of relief.

I had come within an inch of throwing *another* last-minute interception against Arkansas.

I looked at the clock. Three seconds left. Time for one more play. This was it. That was the biggest football moment of my life.

Bud sent in the play. We broke the huddle.

I expect to win, I told myself. *I've got this. Stay loose. Trust yourself.*

My heart was pounding. My hands were sweating.

This is it.

I put my hands under center and looked over the defense. Then I heard whistles. Arkansas had called timeout. They wanted to see the offense we lined up in and make adjustments accordingly.

I welcomed the timeout. I needed to calm down.

On the sidelines, Bud shouted instructions to the team. He called a new play and went over assignments.

As the offense headed back onto the field, Bud pulled me aside and said, "Danny, this is your moment. This is something you've spent your whole life dreaming about. Now, you get to live it. Go out there and make it happen. I believe in you."

I nodded and began trotting to catch up with the rest of the offense.

"And Danny," Bud yelled from behind.

I stopped, turned around, and saw Bud grinning.

"Remember to have fun. It's a game. Enjoy it, baby!"

I smiled, gave Bud a thumbs up, and jogged to the offense waiting in the huddle.

Bud's words calmed me down.

There may have been more than 50,000 fans screaming their heads off. There may have been a conference championship and a trip to the Cotton Bowl on the line. There may have been two exhausted teams and two passionate fanbases hoping and praying for opposite results. But in the end, it was just a game. A great game. A game I loved. A game that was *fun*.

Despite the stakes, there was nowhere else I wanted to be at that moment. I *wanted* the ball in my hands. I *wanted* this opportunity. I was confident I could find the open man and deliver him the ball. I *expected* to win this game.

We broke the huddle.

My heartbeat relaxed. My hands were no longer sweating. I was right where I wanted to be.

I called out the cadence, took the snap, and dropped back to pass.

Arkansas blitzed a linebacker who was now barreling in from my right side. I cut to the left and thought about scrambling out of the pocket, but I knew the odds were long that I could make it the twelve yards to the goal line.

I stopped myself from moving further to the left and saw a defensive lineman breaking free on the left side of my offensive line.

No time to analyze. It was all instincts.

I cut back to the middle of the line while stepping forward to avoid the pressure from the blitzing linebacker on the right. The battle at the line converged around me as I looked upfield.

Time was running out fast. I was about to be sacked. But nobody was open.

Doesn't matter. I've got to give my receiver a chance.

I cocked my right arm back, ready to pass. I couldn't take a sack. I had to throw up a fifty-fifty ball and hope my receiver could fight off his defender and pull it in.

Before I could release the ball, I felt a defender's paw knock into my right forearm. I lost my grip and bobbled the football awkwardly, but I secured it with both hands and didn't drop it.

I had to get out of this mess. I couldn't try to throw it again with Razorback arms swinging at me and grabbing at my jersey.

I took another step upfield and was now dangerously close to crossing the line of scrimmage, which would make it illegal for me to throw a forward pass.

I did the only thing I could. I tucked the ball and ran

forward. It was end zone or bust.

I sprinted past the ten-yard line and cut towards the right side of the field. I saw a defensive back racing towards me from the left.

Reggie saw me running and became a blocker, pushing back a defender in the end zone to my right.

I had to make it to the corner of the end zone. If I could beat the defender pursuing from my left, I'd have a shot at diving across the goal line behind Reggie's block in the end zone. It was all happening so fast.

Get there. Get there.

I crossed the five.

The defender pursuing from my left was too fast. He was taking an angle that would make contact with me just before I reached the goal line.

Meanwhile, the defender in the endzone worked his way free from Reggie's block and was now approaching me from the right, much faster than I expected. I was on track to get sandwiched between the Arkansas players two yards short of the goal line.

No going back now.

I can do it. I can get there.

At the three-yard line, the defender to my right lowered his shoulder and aimed for my hip. The defender to my left came in high, aiming for my torso.

Without thinking, I leaped into the air, diving for the goal line.

I was airborne as the Razorback to my right crashed into my legs, which sent me into a spin just as the defender to my left made contact with my upper body and gave my spin more momentum. I helicoptered in midair, spinning my entire body in a 360-degree turn. On my way down, I managed to extend the ball outward.

I landed on the hard green turf with the ball in my outstretched hands...the nose of the football two inches across the white line that marked the end zone.

I looked to my right and saw the official raise his arms as he blew his whistle. Touchdown.

My nearby teammates piled on me, screaming in celebration before I could get back to my feet. Soon, every player from our sideline had joined us in the end zone.

We did it. We won, 29-28.

We were the new Southwest Conference champions, going from worst to first in three seasons.

After the game, a reporter asked me where I got the confidence to risk running for the score with the game on the line.

I smiled and said, "Coach Sullivan and this staff have been teaching us the power of confidence from the moment they arrived. Three years ago, there's no way I would have had the confidence to do that. Maybe not even three weeks ago. But like Coach says, at some point you just have to decide to be confident. When you do that, good things will happen. Today, good things happened."

41

"Live life with a smile no matter what. It's a powerful choice that you make."

– Dabo Swinney, 2-Time National Champion Football Coach

Saturday Afternoon, August 31, 2019

I'm a few blocks from campus, driving towards Bud Sullivan Stadium with the windows down. Tonight's kickoff is a good five hours away, but I can already smell charcoals burning and barbeque smoking. The gameday smell wafts from the stadium parking lot and envelops the nearby neighborhoods.

As Sherry and I make our way closer to the stadium, I see students sitting on the porches of houses they are renting, talking and laughing with each other, taking in the bright sun. I smile and shake my head. The college life.

Students and adults alike are walking in packs to the stadium, on their way to tailgate parties. Everyone is happy and excited. It's a beautiful college football gameday in

Joline, Arkansas. Life is good.

We hit a traffic slowdown two blocks from the stadium gate we will be entering through. The stadium is within view now. Much larger than it was when I played here. The success Bud Sullivan had during his tenure led to impressive expansions to make room for bigger crowds.

I think back to my final season here. That dramatic finish. That conference championship—Bud's first of several.

About a month after our win against Arkansas, we played in the Cotton Bowl on New Year's Day in 1990. It was a childhood dream come true. In much less dramatic fashion compared to the Arkansas game, we won by fourteen points led by a steady running game and Clarence's three touchdowns. Our defense also played great, allowing just ten points.

In the spring of 1990, I graduated. In the summer, I married Sherry. In the three decades that have since passed, we raised a family and I worked my way into my dream job of hosting a national sports talk radio show.

As for Bud, he turned down multiple offers from bigger schools to stay at Arkansas A&M after the 1989 season. He ended up coaching the Bulldogs for twenty-one years.

Over time, he adapted his offense, becoming one of the first coaches to implement the spread option attack out of the shotgun formation—a concept that has since made its way through all levels of football, including the NFL.

Bud led Arkansas A&M through conference realignment after the Southwest Conference dissolved following the 1995 season. He turned the school into a national power throughout the 1990s and early 2000s, even winning a BCS National Championship along the way.

He retired from coaching after the 2007 season. Only sixty years old at the time, his retirement surprised the college football world. Bud said simply, with that big grin on his face at the press conference announcing his retirement, "When you know, you know. It's my time to step down and do some other things."

He still lives in Joline. He has several successful businesses he's involved with and he continues to be a big part of the university. We're heading to his tailgate party right this moment.

I show my gate pass to the stadium parking attendant and he waves me down the appropriate lane. I follow the signs to a V.I.P. tailgating area with large white tents set up. We park and make our way over to the area where Bud is hosting his party—on this Saturday, the party is reserved for the '89 squad's team reunion.

I flash my laminated pass to an attendant stationed at some ropes that lead to the V.I.P. tents. He nods and says, "I'm a big fan of your show."

I thank him, shake his hand, and let him know how much I appreciate his support.

I enter one of the large tents and I'm greeted by loud

gameday music and dozens of friendly, familiar faces.

Brian Dawson is here. He greets me with a bear hug and goes right into sharing outrageous stories and big laughs, as always. We've stayed tight through the years. Brian was an All-American his senior year, spent seven years in the NFL, and then moved back to Joline, where he still lives today. We always laugh about how badly he wanted to leave this town back when he was in college, only to return as soon as his football career was over. He's now the owner of Dawson Auto Group—a large conglomerate of car dealerships based in Joline, but with new lots expanding all the way to Little Rock. You see his billboards all over town. A natural salesman, it's no surprise he's had lots of success in this line of work.

I catch up with Clarence Washington, the one guy wearing a suit and tie to this event. He has to. He's now the school's athletic director and has work to do on game days. After graduating from Arkansas A&M, Clarence spent nine years in the NFL. When his playing days were over, he came back and got his Master's Degree in Education before embarking on a long career in school and sports administration. He was hired as A&M's A.D. three years ago, coming full circle. He can't stay long at the tailgate, but it's great seeing him.

I spend time talking with Reggie Coleman. He's a high school teacher and coach in Texas. He tells me he made the drive over last night, after his team's season-opening victory.

I also catch up with Michael Murray. He took over as A&M's quarterback in 1990 and had a stellar college career. A knee injury would cut his pro career short, but he has no regrets. He went to law school after his short stint in the NFL, moved back to Joline, and is now partner at the biggest law firm in town.

I catch up with dozens of other former teammates, some I haven't seen since college. Yet, we all pick up right where we left off, just like old times. There's a brotherhood that is formed on tight football teams and you never really lose that comfortable feeling that families tend to have.

When I finally make my way over to Bud, he greets me as he always does with a firm handshake, a smack on the shoulder, and a big laugh.

"Damn good to see you, Danny." Bud is one of the few people who still calls me *Danny* instead of *Dan*.

Bud, his wife, Sherry, and I all start catching up like we always do.

I see Bud about once a year, sometimes more. Every time I'm in town, we get together for lunch or dinner and we've also done our fair share of golf outings over the years. He's always smiling and happy. The man loves life more than just about anyone I know and his joy is contagious.

We talk often on the phone. He's a coach who means it when he says coaching a player doesn't end after four or five years; it's a lifetime commitment to each player.

Over the last three decades, I can't count the times Bud has helped guide me through whatever problem I'm dealing with, usually reminding me of the confidence-building techniques he taught me as a player. He's the greatest mentor I've ever had.

Perhaps it's the nostalgia of being back on campus, thirty years after my last season here, but I can't stop thinking about that 1989 season and how we turned things around so quickly.

When I look at where I was in the fall of 1986, before Bud was hired at Arkansas A&M, and where I am now — it seems unreal. I cringe when I think of how close I was to making the worst decision of my life and dropping out of school. I smile with gratitude when I think of all the lessons I learned from Bud about living life with self-confidence. It's scary to consider how different my life could have turned out.

Bud taught me how to build confidence in myself and he taught me that maintaining confidence requires a lifetime commitment to the techniques he taught.

He also taught me that life is a game and you're supposed to enjoy it. How easy it is to forget that. How easy it is to get overwhelmed and lose sight of the things that are most important.

Whenever I'm around Bud, his very presence serves as a reminder of those lessons. He lives them out.

Kickoff approaches and the tailgate party thins out as

people make their way to the stadium. I have a chance to pull Bud aside and ask him a question that has been on my mind these last two days, returning to the site of one of the most impressive turnarounds in college football history.

"Coach," I say, "there's something I've always meant to ask you. How did you know your philosophy would work here? Why were you so sure you could turn things around? All that talk of confidence seems like it could've blown up in your face."

Bud slapped me on the back. "I knew there were no guarantees, but it's like I always told you boys: **At some point, you just have to decide to be confident. When you do that, good things will happen.**

"If you believe that and you live by that, you're gonna have a whole lot of success in life. And a whole lot of fun. That's exactly what I did. I decided to believe in myself and my philosophy. It has worked out well for me."

He lets out a big laugh and tells me to save him a seat in his suite.

That's Bud. The man is the walking embodiment of self-confidence. He serves as a constant reminder to me that confidence is a choice.

When you choose to be confident, good things happen.

Acknowledgements

To write this book about how to build confidence, I spent months researching many outstanding books, interviews, and studies on the topic. Some of my favorite authors on the topic include Dr. David Schwartz, Dr. Maxwell Maltz, Dr. Bob Rotella, Dr. Shad Helmstetter, Dr. Martin Seligman, and Zig Ziglar — one of the greatest teachers there ever was on the power of self-image.

As always, my work is heavily influenced by the writings and teachings of great coaches and athletes. I want to specifically acknowledge the influential lessons and careers of legendary coaches Barry Switzer, Lou Holtz, Tony Dungy, Augie Garrido, Jimmy Johnson, Mike Krzyzewski, Tommy Lasorda, Vince Lombardi, Buck O'Neil, Pat Riley, Nick Saban, Bill Snyder, Steve Spurrier, Bob Stoops, Dabo Swinney, and John Wooden. Each of these coaches had (or still have) an extraordinary ability to build confidence in their teams.

Because this book was set in the world of college football during the 1980s, it was important for me to spend time interviewing two Hall of Fame coaches who won National

Championships during this era and had reputations for building highly-confident teams. I want to thank Barry Switzer and Lou Holtz for taking the time to personally visit with me about the methods they used to generate confidence in their players. Both of these coaches went above and beyond to answer my questions and I can't thank them enough for the time and wisdom they shared with me.

In particular, I want to acknowledge a few specific concepts featured in this book.

Coach Switzer's "three aspects of the game" along with his firm belief that treating people right and having fun were two components directly tied to achieving success and building confidence had a big influence on the direction of this book.

Coach Holtz's "three rules" for building confidence and the "Sunday night meetings" he implemented in the 1980s — meetings focused solely on teaching self-improvement strategies to his players — were also powerful confidence-building techniques featured in this book.

It was a true honor to spend time with both coaches and I learned a lot about the power of confidence from these two football legends. I can't thank you enough!

About the Author

DARRIN DONNELLY is the bestselling author of *Think Like a Warrior*, *Relentless Optimism*, and several others books in the inspirational *Sports for the Soul* series. Though the main characters in Donnelly's books are usually coaches or athletes, they represent anyone with a big dream and the desire to be successful. The seasons and games they endure represent the seasons of life we all must go through when trying to master a new skill, achieve a new goal, or rebound from a setback.

Sports for the Soul books help readers fill their minds with motivation and positivity while also learning how to build confidence, overcome adversity, and achieve their goals — in all areas of life.

Donnelly lives in Kansas City with his wife and three children. He can be reached at *SportsForTheSoul.com* and on Twitter *@DarrinDonnelly*.

Sports for the Soul

Stories of Faith, Family, Courage, and Character.

This book is part of the *Sports for the Soul* series. For updates on this book, future books, and a free newsletter that delivers advice and inspiration from top coaches, athletes, and sports psychologists, join us at: **SportsForTheSoul.com**.

The *Sports for the Soul* newsletter will help you:

- Find your calling and follow your passion
- Harness the power of positive thinking
- Build your self-confidence
- Attack every day with joy and enthusiasm
- Develop mental toughness
- Increase your energy and stay motivated
- Explore the spiritual side of success
- Be a positive leader for your family and your team
- Become the best version of yourself
- And much more…

Join us at: **SportsForTheSoul.com**.

Collect the previous books in
the Sports for the Soul series...

Visit SportsForTheSoul.com

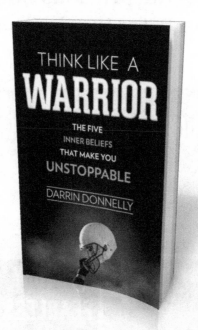

Think Like a Warrior

by Darrin Donnelly

In this bestselling inspirational fable, a college football coach at the end of his rope receives mysterious visits from five of history's greatest coaches: **John Wooden, Buck O'Neil, Herb Brooks, Bear Bryant, and Vince Lombardi**. Together, these legendary leaders teach him the five inner beliefs shared by the world's most successful people. The "warrior mindset" he develops changes his life forever — and it will change yours as well.

Book No. 2 in the *Sports for the Soul* series…

Old School Grit

by Darrin Donnelly

An old-school college basketball coach who thinks like John Wooden and talks like Mike Ditka enters the final NCAA tournament of his legendary career and uses his last days as a coach to write letters to the next generation revealing his rules for a happy and successful life: the 15 rules of grit. Consider this book an instruction manual for getting back to the values that truly lead to success and developing the type of old school grit that will get you through anything.

Book No. 3 in the *Sports for the Soul* series...

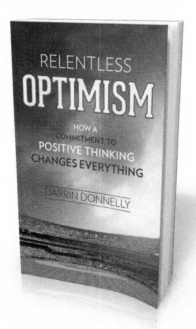

Relentless Optimism
by Darrin Donnelly

A minor-league baseball player realizes his lifelong dream of making it to the majors is finally coming to an end. That is, until he meets an unconventional manager who teaches him that if he wants to change his outcomes in life, he must first change his attitude. This book will show you just how powerful a positive attitude can be and it will teach you how to use positive thinking to make your biggest dreams come true.

Book No. 4 in the *Sports for the Soul* series…

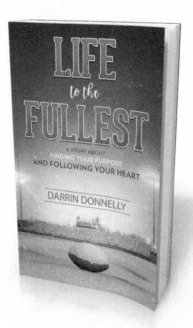

Life to the Fullest
by Darrin Donnelly

This is an inspirational football fable for anyone who has ever struggled to find their purpose or questioned whether it was safe to follow their passion in life. It's a story about fathers and sons. It's a story about faith, family, and community. Most of all, it's a story about having the courage to follow your heart and live your true purpose.

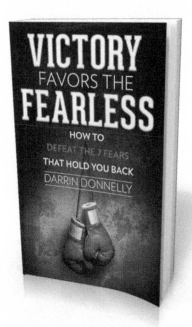

Victory Favors the Fearless

by Darrin Donnelly

A struggling pro boxer learns from a wise trainer that he'll never defeat his opponents in the ring until he first defeats the fears within himself. As this fighter learns to defeat the seven common fears that hold him back, it propels him on a journey that takes him all the way to a championship battle for the ages.

Made in the USA
Monee, IL
02 July 2021

72760464R00163